99 Keys to a Creative Life

About Melissa Harris

An internationally published artist and psychic, Melissa Harris has dedicated her life to the creation of imagery that celebrates life, love, beauty, nature, and magic. She is a Fulbright Scholar recipient in painting and also holds a BFA and an MFA in painting.

Equally sought after for her intuitive and artistic abilities, Melissa travels throughout the country teaching art-making workshops, creativity workshops and classes, and composing her popular Spirit Essence Portraits—unique paintings combining her artistic proficiency and her psychic skills. Her original paintings can be found in numerous private and public collections. As an entrepreneur, she offers fine-art originals and reproductions of her work, as well as a full line of greeting cards and products that are produced by her publishing company, Creatrix. These products include the *Creatrix Anything Is Possible* card deck (also licensed to Koppenhol in Holland) and her autobiographical *Painting Outside the Lines: The Life of Psychic Artist Melissa Harris*, a full-color book that showcases seventy-eight of her paintings. Her art has been featured on many books, CD covers, and calendars, as well as in the *Goddess on the Go* card deck (published by AG Mueller in Switzerland and U.S. Games in the United States) and the 2011 *Anything Is Possible* sixteen-month wall calendar (Trends International). Her images continue to inspire people of all ages to journey into the Divine Feminine and find their sacred dreams.

Melissa enjoys getting out into the world and connecting with people. She is a popular exhibitor at festivals, trade shows, and conferences. You will find her lecturing on creativity, holding workshops, and painting Spirit Essence Portraits at these conferences as well as in gift stores and holistic centers including Omega Institute. With thousands of clients across the country, Melissa travels from her home outside of Woodstock, New York, to Arizona, California, Colorado, Minnesota, Virginia, Massachusetts, New Hampshire, Pennsylvania, Maine, Florida, and Hawaii. For more information on Melissa, and to purchase any of her products, visit www.melissaharris.com.

99 Keys to a Creative Life

Spiritual, Intuitive, and Awareness Practices
for Personal Fulfillment

MELISSA HARRIS

Llewellyn Publications
Woodbury, Minnesota

FIRST EDITION
First Printing, 2015

Book design by Bob Gaul
Cover and part page art by www.iStockphoto.com/40767092/©ArtLana
Cover design by Ellen Lawson
Editing by Ed Day

"Using Rejection as a Catalyst" was originally published in *Painting Outside the Lines: The Life of Psychic Artist Melissa Harris* (copyright) 2012.

Llewellyn Publications is a registered trademark of Llewellyn Worldwide Ltd.

Library of Congress Cataloging-in-Publication Data
Harris, Melissa, 1955–
  99 keys to a creative life: spiritual, intuitive and awareness
practices for personal fulfillment/Melissa Harris.—First edition.
      pages cm
    ISBN 978-0-7387-4219-9
1. Creative ability. 2. Creative thinking. 3. Self-actualization (Psychology)
4. Intuition. 5. Spirituality. I. Title. II. Title: Ninety-nine keys to a creative life.
  BF408.H3153 2015
  153.3'5—dc23
                              2014047875

Llewellyn Worldwide Ltd. does not participate in, endorse, or have any authority or responsibility concerning private business transactions between our authors and the public.
    All mail addressed to the author is forwarded but the publisher cannot, unless specifically instructed by the author, give out an address or phone number.
    Any Internet references contained in this work are current at publication time, but the publisher cannot guarantee that a specific location will continue to be maintained. Please refer to the publisher's website for links to authors' websites and other sources.

Llewellyn Publications, a Division of Llewellyn Worldwide Ltd.
2143 Wooddale Drive
Woodbury, MN 55125-2989
www.llewellyn.com
Printed in the United States of America

Table of Contents

Dedication   xvii

Acknowledgments   xix

Introduction   1

....

Awareness Keys:
***Heads Up! Creative Opportunities
Are All Around Us!***

    1. Breathe   13

    2. Define Success   14

    3. Set Intentions   16

    4. Inner or Outer Audience?   17

    5. Seek Inspiration   19

6. Document   21

7. Make Time for Play!   23

8. Nurturing/Honoring Curiosity   25

9. Sound Healing   26

10. Take a Class   28

11. Conducive Surroundings   30

12. Practice Mindfulness   32

13. Creative Cycles   33

14. Responsibility   35

15. Positive Vibes   36

16. Monitoring Your Energy   38

17. Visual Influence   40

18. Repetitive Viewing   42

19. Color Attraction   44

20. Enjoy the Creations of Others   46

21. Network   47

22. Judgment   48

23. Accepting Advice   50

24. Helping Out   52

25. Speak Up!   54

26. Listen to Your Body   55

27. Take a Break   57

28. Fuel   59

29. Location Inspiration   61

30. Cultural Diversity   63

31. Fun with Children   64

32. Choices   66

33. Commitment   67

....

Intuitive or Heart-Based Keys:
Allow Your Inner Compass to Guide You.

34. Tune In!   75

35. Deep Listening   77

36. Be Receptive   79

37. Send   81

38. Contemplation   83

39. Dream Work   85

40. Be Flexible   88

41. Ask/Listen   90

42. Honor Your Hunches   92

43. Social Intuiting   93

44. Let's Pretend   94

45. Automatic Writing   96

46. Chaos as a Creative Force   97

47. Creative Shutdown   99

48. Compromise   101

49. The Right-Brain Experience   103

50. Jumping In   104

51. Experiment with Different Mediums   106

52. Let the Work Guide You   108

53. Gifting   110

54. Completion   111

55. Collaborate   113

56. Inner Knowing   114

57. Sticky Situations   116

58. Magical Tools   118

59. Psychometry   120

60. Shifting Focus   121

61. Letting Go   123

62. Dress Deliberately   124

63. Pet Communication   126

64. On the Fly   127

65. Pay It Forward   129

66. As in Life, So in Art   130

....

Spiritual or Soul-Based Keys:
Establish or Strengthen Your
Connection to the Divine.

67. Meditate   139

68. Creative Prayer   141

69. Open to Spirit   143

70. Gratitude   145

71. Grace   146

72. The Power of Humility   148

73. The Soul and the Personality   150

74. Be Seen   151

75. Be Courageous   153

76. Triggers   154

77. Embracing Vulnerability   157

78. Receiving   159

79. Boundaries   160

80. Clearing   162

81. Self-Nurturing   164

82. Mentor   165

83. Patience   167

84. Anger   169

85. Rejection   171

86. Decisions   173

87. Volunteer   175

88. Journaling   177

89. Vision Board   178

90. Read   180

91. Create Altars   181

92. Celebrate Your Creations   183

93. Dance!   185

94. Physical Movement   186

95. Feng Shui (Sacred Space)   188

96. Nature   190

97. Empowerment   192

98. Self-Love   194

99. Unconditional Love   196

Conclusion   201

Recommended Resources   205

Dedication

This book is dedicated to those who believe or have been told they are not creative and yearn to exercise that part of their being. We are all creative. Enjoy using this book to open your imagination.

Acknowledgments

The subject of this book addresses exactly where I've shined a spotlight in my life. First of all, I'd like to thank Angela Wix at Llewellyn for finding me at an expo and inviting me to write a book about my life focus. It was meant to be! A special thank you to the staff at Llewellyn for all of your assistance with this project. Much of what I have learned and applied in my everyday and spiritual life are tools that I learned from the Pathwork lectures. The 258 Pathwork Guide lectures were transmitted for many years through the spiritual channel of Eva Pierrakos. These teachings were brought by a spirit entity who is known as "the Guide." A big thank you goes out to Eva, The Guide, and all who were involved in spreading the wisdom found in these teachings. I could not complete any project that involves writing without the help of Ja-lene Clark, a creative genius and writer herself, who works magic by helping others extract content and turn it into a finished work. A big thank also you goes out to Joanne Sprott for her precise editing skills. Thanks to Kent Robison for his tireless help in running errands, doing chores, cat-keeping, wood-piling, and general support. Thank you to my dad, Donald Harris, for his love and support. I appreciate all of you who discouraged me from becoming an artist by profession because in doing that you helped me to connect with my inner strength and determination. Finally, thank you to all of you whom I've encountered in my love of the creative process, including both my teachers and my students, because we are all each others' teachers. Whoops, and thanks to Timmy the cat who kept me company right on the keypad during the entire writing of the book.

Introduction

One of my greatest joys in life is to help folks develop their creativity. I'm amazed at the number of people who tell me that they were discouraged from their various creative efforts while in elementary or high school. Perhaps they were told they were not good at drawing, someone may have laughed at their book report, or they did not excel in glee club but wanted very much to sing.

We are especially vulnerable to criticism during our school years. Being told that we are not creative may result in scars that can take years of inner work to overcome. Too much criticism can stifle creativity for life. In teaching my art-making workshops, I take great joy in watching those who have stayed away from art for years and, with great trepidation, have found the courage to attend. I watch as they tiptoe into their artwork and gradually become more confident as the workshop progresses. Even if some students do not continue to make art, they have conquered a demon by showing up to create. Facing our fears is empowering.

If you are already trained and ensconced in your creative process, these keys can help you to refine and dig even deeper into your infinite well of creativity. For those who consider yourselves creatives but have been away from your craft because you are blocked, these keys can serve as tools to help reactivate your creative juices. If you have never considered yourself creative, my hope is that you open to new ways of defining creativity and discover rich resources within yourself.

In *99 Keys to a Creative Life*, I invite you to discover that when you censor your thoughts and ideas and too easily discount them as unworthy of consideration, you continue the vicious cycle of shutting down what could be a great idea before it is even hatched. When we close down, our energy weakens, self-doubt creeps in, and we reinforce all those false notions that we aren't able to or don't deserve to access our own creativity.

The many small acts we perform daily on a rote, mechanical basis for ourselves and others can be the gateway for learning to view small, seemingly ordinary details in different ways. Other times it is our inner focus that allows us to employ our creative faculties to begin to shift our lives in the directions that will allow more happiness. My goal in writing this book is to help you find your creative gateways by using these keys to establish new routines or thought patterns to support or exercise creativity.

Creativity is not just painting, writing, or making something tangible that we see, hear, or touch. Creativity is stepping outside of the way we normally think or act, and this allows us to look at many situations from different angles. It's a state of being that we can apply virtually all day long to transcend our usual way of looking at our inner and outer worlds. It can also be described as a muscle: the more we use it, the more naturally and easily it works on its own. To strengthen this ability, we must use our will and desire to bring our creative attention into focus as often as we can.

I've been creating for as long as I can remember. According to my parents, the only way to shut me up was to give me some crayons and paper. When I tired of that, I would go outside and "lose myself" in nature. I'd sit up in the top of a tall tree for hours, tuning in to the birds, insects, clouds, and whatever else happened to come my way. Episodes of clairvoyance were sprinkled into both my days and my dreamtime.

In my early twenties, I immersed myself in the world of metaphysics and began channeling just a few years later. The channeling sessions turned into hands-on healing sessions in which I was instructed by my guides to place my hands over sections of folks' bodies and make different sounds, a technique we now refer to as toning. I enrolled in the Barbara Brennan School of Healing to learn more about what I was being called to do.

Because I could not make time for both the energy healing *and* my art, for many years I turned my full attention onto my artistic career. However, because the role of healer is a large part of who I came here to be, I knew that I would find my way to connecting both of these aspects of my being. Over time, I found ways to combine my skills in my art-making classes as well as by publishing cards, prints, calendars, and other items featuring imagery with the intention of inspiring others. I returned to psychic reading sessions and added the option of illustrating what I see in a session into a personal painting that I call a Spirit Essence Portrait. In *99 Keys to a Creative Life* I offer you all of the information, tips, shortcuts, and tools I discovered along the way.

In this book I also share with you the spiritual, intuitive, and awareness practices that I use to keep and expand my creative edge. My experiences and the training I received in my life path as a spiritual student and teacher, healer, psychic, empath, and artist are coalesced into this book. I offer intriguing ways to apply spirituality to your creative process as well as provide ideas about applying spiritual principles to enhance or improve your individual connection to Spirit.

How to Use This Book

I've divided the book into three sections because these three aspects are essential in order to expand our capacity to create. You can use the book in a variety of ways. You may want to select the section where you feel strongest and proceed from there. For example, if you already know that your intuitive capabilities are working for you, this is a great place to begin because you already have a strong foundation. Or you may pick and read a single key if you only have a moment. Concentrate on one section until you feel confident. Alternatively, you can just read the book front to back if you like. Move along at your own pace; refer to it often.

All practices emphasize how our creative power lies within ourselves. In preparation for your journey, I highly recommend that you have on hand a camera, a journal or notebook, and possibly a device to record sound; all are good tools for creative souls.

You too can unlock the gate to a more creative life. This book is for those who are already creative and want to find a new level of fulfillment *and* for beginners at whatever age embarking on a new creative path. These keys to creativity hold the power to bring you to a new level of inspiration, happiness, and joy. Our daily practices can transform the ordinary into the extraordinary and grant us the opportunity to live life at a high level of personal fulfillment. Enjoy the journey!

AWARENESS KEYS:

Heads Up!
Creative Opportunities
Are All Around Us!

It's easy to get so lost in holding together our busy, sometimes chaotic lives—carpool, school, work, daycare, dinner, holidays—that we end up ignoring what else is in our immediate path. If we are constantly preoccupied with the next task or busy worrying, we may not notice the landscape we just passed that might make a great painting, or the song on the radio that could inspire the creation of a new character in our novel. These gifts could be inspirations for creative ideas as well as opportunities for inner growth. That argument you just had with a coworker could be turned on its head and become a positive experience by using your awareness to take a deep look at all sides of the situation. By doing so, you may come to an understanding of where you may need to grow and stretch to help in your personal development.

Awareness means being awake and present so that you recognize even the subtle things that can either stifle or propel you. These are mental, emotional, and physical keys to help you become more attentive, which can prepare you to make choices leading to greater creativity. In this section, we consider many aspects of our lives and follow our creative urges even in the smallest of actions to help make creativity a habit. We learn to observe how the ordinary is transformed into the extraordinary and become able to fully enjoy the creations of others. Our commitment to awareness can show Spirit we have made a decision to live at a high level of personal and creative fulfillment.

I used to be guilty of daydreaming to the degree that it was detrimental to getting things accomplished. When I was in school, my mind was hardly ever on my studies because I was busy thinking about getting out and going to play, and later busy thinking about what I wanted to paint. In fact, I stood a book up on my small desk and hid a drawing behind it, not even taking part in the subject of the class. My grades were low in the subjects that didn't hold my attention, as you can imagine.

Later in life, I realized that this ingrained habit of allowing my mind to wander was not serving me well and decided to address the problem. I put effort into harnessing where my awareness was at any given moment. I was surprised at how often my mind was elsewhere once I began making it a habit to do some of the exercises found in the keys in this section. You too should be able to notice rather quickly that your mind strays less and you are staying on task, getting things done in a more efficient manner. It may take a few months to notice changes, depending on your attentiveness, but don't get discouraged; your reward of a greater ability to focus is well worth it. These exercises are especially helpful when we are in a period of emotional distress.

Awareness practices deepen our ability to know what enhances our creativity and fosters inner peace. Awareness forms a base, a platform, from which we can develop the keys in all of the sections. (The Intuitive and Spiritual keys in the book start with awareness.) If you are functioning with maximum consciousness, things will fall into place with greater ease, and your creative faculties will soar because you are present to open to inspiration and to receiving incoming ideas. Awareness calls us to open our eyes, ears, heart, and mind. When we are alert we are available to receive creative inspiration from infinite sources. We are taking care of our health, responsibilities, and relationships so that we are free from "clutter." Working with the keys in this section will help remove obstacles and clear your path to optimum flow in your creations. We take more responsibility in our relationships when we are aware of energy dynamics with others.

These keys ask you to focus on your surroundings, relationships or your physical health. All of these are factors in how available we are to receive creative inspiration and put it into motion. If we are walking around in a fog, we miss much of what could be integrated into a more creative life. If we surrender to participating in relationships that are no longer working, we lose life-force energy. And, if we are living and/or working in surroundings that don't make us feel good, we can make use of this opportunity to create happy spaces.

The creations of others can have a positive impact on our own creations. Are you getting out enough, reading enough, and listening enough to know what you enjoy and what inspires you? Are you following any curious urges that could lead to greater creative fulfillment?

Imagine beginning your day by putting on a pair of eyeglasses that sharpen everything that comes your way. Awareness is yours with a bit of effort and focus. Enjoy the benefits of having things fall into place with much less effort. Your creative endeavors will blossom with more abundance and power because you are awake and aware! Hooray!

1. Breathe

Breathing—it seems like something we shouldn't have to contemplate. It's automatic, a given; one less thing to address—right? Actually, no. Most people are not tuned into their breath at all and take it for granted. The simple awareness of our breath can improve our mental and physical health. For example, have you ever caught yourself holding your breath? Were you aware of why you were doing that? You can use the breath to send your attention and energy to certain parts of your body. In this way, you can increase the awareness of your body, as well as stimulate healing energy.

Emotions affect our breathing patterns. As you move through your day, begin to notice what is happening in your body as you experience different feelings. When I am fearful or anxious, I tend to hold my breath. Nothing moves; a sort of paralysis sets in. Bringing my awareness to my breath and allowing it to move through as much of my body as possible brings an immediate sense of relief. To accelerate the healing process, I imagine I am breathing through any part of my body that needs healing. Alternatively, I notice that when I am excited or happy I automatically breathe more deeply. When I am relaxed, it is easier for me to settle down into my creative process. If I am worried, I dwell upon the subject that caused my concerns, which decreases my desire to create and hinders my ability to settle in and concentrate on a project.

Fortunately, there are many venues for teaching us to engage with our breath. Almost all physical exercise, and especially martial arts and yoga, emphasize and utilize good breathing habits. I especially recommend kundalini yoga because the main focus is on the breath. If you are experiencing stress, consider either working with breath exercises or participating in a physical activity before you address your creative venture.

Learn to tune in and maintain an awareness of how your breath is circulating throughout your body. Once you master this awareness you will have a greater feeling of well-being and enhanced productivity, which can accelerate your creativity.

2. Define Success

How do you define success? It is easy to get trapped into defining our success with dollars, prestige, or the number of CDs sold. Is success completing your CD, novel, or painting? Is success having other people admire you or your work? Is victory the number of units sold? Many of us are taught to believe that money equals success, but I have come across many wealthy folks who are not at all satisfied with their lives. I encourage you to contemplate how *you* define success—*your* opinion is the most important one. Perhaps it is having a peaceful home life, enough resources to travel, satisfying friendships, or beautiful surroundings. These components are popular with many, but this is an individual question for each of us, to define our own unique formula for success.

If you are not sure about what success means for you, take a single week of your life and journal each day, noticing the highs and lows and how you handle those feelings. You will begin to discover patterns and hopefully come to a clear understanding of what is most important to you. You may find during this week that the situations or interactions that brought you the most joy were not what you would have expected. Use that information as a tool for redefining or refining what makes your heart sing. It may be as simple as discovering that you have found a new ability to communicate in a clear way with a friend or associate. It may be that you were able to hit a note on your musical instrument that was previously inaccessible. Or perhaps you found yourself able to understand some technology that seemed way too complex prior to this effort.

Since ideally we are always growing and changing, the ways in which we define success will also shift. Are you able to flow with these shifts or are you stuck on old ideas of what you thought you wanted to create? There is a freedom that goes along with flexibility in allowing continued change.

Acknowledge your successes. No matter the size of each positive movement forward, they are *your* successes. Appreciate them! By defining success for yourself, you will be able to use your creativity to develop your own version of a successful life.

3. Set Intentions

Our creations start with setting intentions. Get very clear on what you want to create and set your intention to do that.

I often ask folks to share three things that they would like to create in their lives, be it material goods or otherwise, and I am surprised at the number of people who have not thought about it. I wrote the following on one of my greeting cards called Spinning Our Dreams—"*How can we manifest our dreams until we know what they are? This was a question that occurred to me a while back. And so I sat down to spin my web of dreams.*"

Become clear about what changes you desire to bring about in your life, if any. If your desires are not foremost in your mind, take time to turn within and journal about what comes up for you when pondering this question. Or you may be completely content in life—marvelous! Your intention may be to get creative about how you may best serve others.

Once you have set your intentions, take whatever steps are necessary to bring these to fruition. Sometimes we find that we are immobilized. This can happen due to fear of failure or not knowing what to do. You may not see your way to the proverbial finish line but most likely you will be able to figure out one tiny movement toward your goal. Journaling about this will help you chart your progress. Sometimes we think nothing is happening, but when we have a way to review our successes, we can be surprised at what we have accomplished.

Creativity comes into play in the steps we take to move forward. Put on your creativity cap, sit down, and set clear intentions!

4. Inner or Outer Audience?

Before you even begin a creative project, take a moment to consider your audience. If you are working on a commissioned project, you obviously need to work with another person's tastes in mind. By accepting a commission you have already made a decision that you are willing to please someone, even if the resulting project may not be your ideal creation. Creating for others is great—as long as we are aware that is what we are doing. However, there may be old voices drifting around in your psyche that you may not be conscious of that are influencing your creativity.

When I began my greeting card company, I started by publishing the images that *I* liked—never considering what would actually sell. I learned the hard way that what I like is far from what tends to sell the best because the images that I gravitate toward are the darker, deeper, more intense paintings with lots of mystery. In a greeting card, folks are usually looking for something light and uplifting. Before I started this company, I had never considered what the audience desired.

As time passed, the images that I painted for myself (without greeting cards in mind) became more self-conscious, less loose and free, because I had become accustomed to thinking about who would be seeing them and at this point, if they might sell. There is something to be said for the saying "dance like no one is watching" because in doing so there is artistic freedom. A subtle strength is reflected in the work that easily emerges when one is not thinking about an audience. My own work tends to be better when I just paint what I feel called to paint. However, if I am working on a commission, having as much information about the desired outcome helps to guide me.

Another aspect to knowing who you are creating for is freeing yourself of unhealthy past influences. Perhaps you were criticized in ways that make you hesitant to express yourself. The feedback that you received in the past may not be relevant to your current creations. I encourage you to become aware of any past judgments concerning your efforts in order to be able to let go and open to what wants to emerge *now*.

The next time you are ready to launch an idea take a moment to review whether or not there are any extraneous voices influencing your creation. This key helps you to achieve and maintain clarity about what you truly want to express.

5. Seek Inspiration

Are you aware of what inspires you? The first few times I was asked, it took me a few moments to gather my response. It was a good question because it helped me to better understand exactly what had gotten my creative juices flowing. My inspirations vary, but some of the core ingredients remain the same.

When we are going through life in a routine manner, we can miss the simplest of delights such as the first birdsong at the end of winter. You may put on a yellow shirt and not even recognize that you are doing it because of the bright forsythia blossoming outside your window. Make creative use of the simple things in your day to open to more creativity.

As you move about your day, notice what catches your eye or ear. Do you watch morning talk shows as you prepare for your day? Have you learned of something there that you may want to follow up on? If so, did you make note of it? Does the color of the news broadcaster's outfit inspire you to dress in a similar manner? Have you seen a commercial for a film or performance you may want to attend? Or do you prefer silence, possibly meditation, as you move into your day, allowing for thoughts to rise from your still waking consciousness? Has the beauty of how the light falls on the windowsill caused you to stop and enjoy it? Has the flock of geese you've seen on your way home from work, signaling the coming of winter, given you pause to reflect upon the season and the emotions it can evoke?

Visuals can help inspire. Enjoy having a look around the social media site Pinterest. Create your own board and keep a running list of things that inspire you—you may even classify it as "inspirations."

If you are having difficulty connecting to your inspirations jot down your thoughts about what has inspired you in the past. Keep your list handy and add to it. You can refer to this list when you are looking for your ongoing creative ideas.

Enjoy a variety of creative insights as you use this key to increase your enjoyment of daily life.

6. Document

I recommend carrying a camera, notebook, or tape recorder with you *everywhere*. These are powerful resources to keep on hand and inspire our creativity. If you are a visual artist, you might create an accordion file to store photos for future inspiration. Musicians can record and store sounds in their environments to weave into recordings later. Writers, carry a notebook with you and be ready to take notes!

As a painter, I am always open to what may be material of interest for future paintings. My friends know what is occurring when I exclaim, "Pull over right now!" when something catches my eye. If I can't stop to paint, I'll take a photo and keep it on hand for later. I've learned the hard way that it is easy to miss opportunities. When I've returned back to a landscape that I wanted to paint, the light may be entirely different and not inspiring at all.

I use my gathered resources as fuel at the times when I am in between painting series and confronting the proverbial white canvas—I can pull out my helpful accordion file of photos I keep for just that reason. My file is divided into sections that make sense for me: butterflies, wild animals, clouds, and more. I could be in the middle of a painting that needs an additional something and even though I may not have plans for what that something is, I pull out my handy file and by flipping through images I get ideas.

I have a musician friend, Lorah Yaccarino, who records sounds wherever she goes, even if the sounds are not "musical." She uses those sounds in her compositions in a variety of creative ways. I particularly enjoyed hearing how she integrated an old recording of street sounds from the tough, drug-dealing section of the old Lower East Side of New York City into a backdrop of sound in a theatrical production.

As a teacher, I stay alert for ideas that may serve as themes for my art-making workshops. Sometimes it can simply be a topic that is mentioned in a casual conversation that I may find myself inspired to use in an upcoming course. Or, someone may make a point about their creative process, so I take note of that and apply it to my students in future classes if there is a connection. My dreams may also provide ideas for paintings, so I write down the content as well as making sketches. Sometimes I develop these sketches into paintings. I carry a notebook in my car in a spot that is easy to reach in case I have an idea, or perhaps hear a song I may want to use in teaching. I never know when things will come in handy.

If you are aware of what is exciting to you, what sparks that "Oh, that would be great as a _____," you will never be at a loss for inspiration with your handy recorded reference library.

7. Make Time for Play!

Vacations, days off, play dates; all of these allow distance from our everyday lives, giving us a chance to wind down and take time for enjoyment. When we are caught up in routines, we can forget to allow for pleasure. It's often in our "off" time that we are most open to what stimulates us in new ways. Here we become aware of activities that make us happy. Make a commitment to block out time for them. Go play!

Some of you may be "routine types" by nature. Many feel most comfortable living life within some sort of structure. Structure can provide a sense of safety, organization, and peace. However, we can find ourselves stuck in a rut without realizing it. Are you able to easily recall the last time that you did something out of the ordinary for yourself? I recognized long ago that making time for play goes a long way in terms of stimulating my creative process. Because I work at home, it's important for me to see and interact with others in order to keep my creativity alive. I am always interested in what makes people who they are and have integrated that curiosity into my work in both direct and indirect ways. I also enjoy observing people's personalities by being a part of a long-running poker game. I'm pretty adept at sorting out a mean poker face!

For me, pleasure does not necessarily mean extravagance or a large-budget activity. Are you aware of what constitutes "fun" in your life, whether it is spending time with family, reading a favorite mystery author, or seeing an adventure film? Maybe seeing your friends is what brings you the most joy, or taking the time to follow an enticing new recipe.

When I know that I have a block of empty time, I have to make sure to schedule an activity that is pleasurable for me so that I have plenty in my "re-charge" bank of fun activities from which to draw. Because I have my own business, I can easily stay involved in what needs to be done, so I actually schedule in activities in the "downtime" blocks.

What brings *you* joy? If you don't have something planned in the near future, walk over to your datebook now and schedule something in!

8. Nurturing/Honoring Curiosity

I was once walking through some gorgeous public gardens with a friend. It was a hot day and she had had enough. I was hot too, but there was an area to our right that was calling to me strongly. I had to listen. As we rounded the curve, we came upon what turned out to be the best, most magical, enchanting section of our entire tour. I took photos to work from later—photos that I know I will end up using in various ways through the next few years. I honored my curiosity...I just had to know what was around that curve, and it paid off!

Curiosity can be the guide to your next creative project. Allow yourself to follow your inquisitive urges. In this key, we learn how following these urges can foster our creativity. Creativity is essentially a "calling" and our callings are guides to new directions or expansions of old ones.

Perhaps you have wondered how an artist gets that loose, effortless effect in a watercolor painting—or how a sound is produced in a song you like. Or maybe you admire a piece of garden art you've come across. It's often easier for us to research questions within our own field of expertise, but when we step outside our normal zone, we sometimes discover gifts that end up feeding other areas of our lives. I'm not very experienced with a hammer and drill, but the times I've wanted to figure out how to craft something have been the proverbial "mother of invention" for me. I have met many women as well as men who enjoy wandering the aisles of hardware stores, letting their minds wander as to how they can apply the gizmos they are curious about. If you have a garden and are imagining how a new plant may look in the midst of what you have established—follow your urge and enjoy your new view.

Sometimes fear precedes our curiosity. Maybe we want to explore a new medium or learn to tango, but we find that fear is getting in the way. I suggest becoming aware of what stops you if your interest is beckoning you to something and you are not answering the call.

I'm notoriously curious, and most of the time it has served me well. We can't know how something may work until we follow our curious urges to explore. Embrace your curiosity as a helpful tool.

9. Sound Healing

My father used to drive my siblings and me crazy with his constant singing. When I asked my mother why it didn't bother her, she replied that singing was his way of keeping his spirits up. Not that one could make a literal comparison, but by looking at how the slaves in this country kept themselves going with their gospel songs, it's easier for me to understand. I'm not a singer myself but I have noticed that if I am in a cheery mood, I might find myself singing.

What role does sound play in your life? Are you one to put on music as you move through your day? Do you listen to the radio or CDs when driving? Perhaps you put on soothing music in the morning to start the day or late at night when you want to wind down. I have friends with insomnia who use soft music to lull themselves to sleep. Do you look forward to the sound of birds chirping as a sign of spring after the long quiet of winter? Does the sound of your cat purring bring a smile to your face? Call in your awareness to understand what you are choosing, when you choose it, and why. This will provide you with a better understanding of how you use sound. I've known writers who listened to all sorts of music, including Led Zeppelin, to help put them into a welcoming state so that they could best receive their creative inspiration. I rarely paint without music. I choose specific tunes from a wide range of styles, but they all help keep me in a sort of trance state so that the ideas keep flowing.

Singing, toning, chanting, playing crystal bowls and gongs, and drumming are great tools for well-being. Various kinds of singing bowls and gongs are popular tools that work with different vibratory frequencies in order to bring about healing. I have attended many concerts with the bowls and found myself "journeying" or in an altered state during the sessions. For days afterward, I felt slightly changed in some way, usually lighter. I enjoy the process of surrendering to where the sounds will take me. However, sound healing is not limited to just gongs and bowls. We can use virtually any instrument, including the voice, as long as the frequencies are helpful to healing. Try humming a favorite uplifting tune if you are feeling down, and see if that simple action might lift your mood.

Be aware of what sounds you are drawn to, when you notice them, and why, for greater understanding about how you can use sound to enhance your well-being or prepare for creativity.

10. Take a Class

Is there an art or a skill calling to you that you continue to put off learning? I have felt nervous walking into a class that I suspect will challenge me. I tend to be shy and the vulnerability of being seen in a position where I am a beginner can be daunting. Many of us are hard on ourselves especially when the fear of failure about our chosen activity can send us swirling into a downward spiral of shame.

Many of us are afraid to learn new skills because the unknown can be intimidating. We may be afraid we won't be able to grasp what is being taught—that we are somehow not good enough. Taking risks is a great way to stretch, and when we stretch we grow.

In my classes, I teach that it's the process not the product. Like most things, usually the apprehension and assumptions about making the choice to take a class are inevitably worse than the reality. I have taken many classes, both in school situations and in workshop atmospheres, and have always taken *something* away, even if I didn't pursue the subject. An awareness of *why* you have chosen a particular topic may be helpful. The decision to take a class has given you insight into a part of you that is looking to expand. The subject you have chosen may be completely new or foreign to you but follow your feeling to explore. If you know that you like to cook, that awareness may lead you to an enticing class in Indian cooking.

For me, the other people I meet in classes are an additional bonus. I may discover the gift of a new friend and/or someone that can offer other information, teachers, or locations for studying that particular subject. In addition, choosing to take yourself out of your ordinary routine can be inspiring in itself. New environments and people can be stimulating!

When we are inspired in one area, it can feed into other areas, providing us with renewed zest for living. Enjoy the results of enriching your life with newfound talents by taking a class. You will enjoy more self-confidence as a result of your new skills. See what else might happen when you open yourself to a new set of skills.

11. Conducive Surroundings

Have you set up your home, office, and/or studio in a way that inspires you? Consider whether or not your surroundings are supporting your creative flow.

Why not take the time to create an environment that best fosters a good flow of imagination? Let's splurge on those flowers if they lift our spirits and put us in the right frame of mind. Perhaps adding an essential-oil diffuser to generate a scent that relaxes you might help maximize productivity. A fountain creating the sound of bubbling water is also soothing. Going the extra mile to create an environment that fosters your creative flow will pay off. Are you aware of what is aesthetically pleasing to you? What colors, fabrics, and types of art do you enjoy? I find that looking at the right piece of art can serve as an ongoing inspiration. "Art" can be whatever you find inspirational. Some people like black-and-white photos, while others might prefer a nice three-dimensional piece or

bright, expressive abstract paintings. You may consider refer-
ring to feng shui principles to focus on specific goals. Even
the color of your walls creates a certain mood, so be sure to
see if that is a mood that is currently serving your creative
drive. If a bookshelf is blocking a window and taking away
some outside light, perhaps you can move it to a different
spot or acquire a shorter piece to bring in more light.

Do you have numerous piles on your desk and overflow-
ing trash bins that result in frantic searches for the document
you need? Even if you are convinced that you do your best
work surrounded by "piles," I suggest experimenting with
cleaning house and keeping it clean and clear for a couple of
weeks. You might notice that you waste less time searching
for papers, or find that you have fewer clutter-related mis-
haps, such as missing a bill payment or getting paperwork
in on time. Organization can create a sense of peace. Do you
have tools for organization such as proper shelving and files?
Is your desk set up in an ergonomically correct fashion? Get
creative!

Creating an optimal atmosphere is a work of art in itself.
Whether flowers or mayhem inspire you, take your imagination beyond your normal limits and construct an environment that fosters creativity and well-being.

12. Practice Mindfulness

While taking your yoga class, you should not think about what you will eat for dinner. Being mindful means being completely present in the moment. How do you define "being present?" When we are present, we are not distracted by the past, the future, or even that very moment. Our focus is on our in-the-moment state of circumstances, and we gain a greater awareness of our surroundings by way of all our senses.

Choose a simple daily activity such as doing the dishes, preparing a meal, taking a shower, etc. During that time, practice being completely present with each sensation, touch, sound, appearance, or taste without allowing yourself to think about the past or future. Feel the dense weight and the smooth surface of your plate as you wash it. Notice the feeling of the warm water on your skin as it rinses the plate clean. Use this practice as a means of mindfulness training.

Yoga is an ideal tool for helping develop mindfulness because we are forced to hold our focus on the physical body as we hold poses. While in a very physically challenging yoga pose, we are not concerned about a problem at work. We are available to notice each sensation in our body, such as the moment our muscles relax into a posture or how we are able to work with our breath to let go more deeply into a pose. Other martial arts are equally helpful.

Being mindful of the physical world around us helps us prevent accidents. If you are noticing the street or path in front of you instead of dwelling on a past event or thinking about a future outing, you are less likely to slip and fall.

Rewards of mindfulness touch every area of our lives. When we are present in any given moment we are open to receive inspirations that may feed our creativity.

13. Creative Cycles

Are you familiar with having a preference for certain activities at particular times of the day or year? Identifying your cycles can be very helpful so that you can make the most of the time you allow for your creative projects.

My own creative urges have shifted over the years. I used to feel my creativity at all different times of the day. For the past several years, though, I have felt like painting or writing mostly in the mornings or afternoons, but occasionally I will feel a pull to go into my studio in the evening. If you are not an "artist" per se, it is still important for you to become familiar with your cycles in order to make the most of your creativity in your everyday life. Here are a few hints:

Creative Cooking

Perhaps you notice that you like to cook early in the day instead of at night? Maybe you are at work at the office and get inspired to make a certain dish for dinner but are too tired. You could consider trying some new recipes in the middle of the day on a weekend day and freezing them for the week.

Morning Songbirds

Maybe you are an early bird musician, but your neighbors would not be enthusiastic about hearing you practice at 6 a.m. Use that morning time to plan where you may play your next gig or mentally explore new compositions and collaborations. If this is really your time to play and experiment, consider honoring your craft by staying at a different location once in a while to make it happen.

Seasons of Creativity

Consider the seasons when you are looking for your best creative times. Some enjoy hunkering down into the dark, short days of winter and using that time to go inside both personally and physically in order to bring forth their most potent creations. If your garden is your canvas, let your creativity explode as you rejoice in plotting out color and shape in your garden.

If you are not sure of your cycles, begin by choosing what creative activity you would like to focus on and do that at different times of the day.

Make a commitment to honor *your* calling when you know your energy is prime for that and see how your creativity improves. Rewards from this awareness will be a better use of your time, bringing you a sense of satisfaction and peace.

14. Responsibility

Since I am a morning person, I take care of the most undesirable activities early in the day when I am fresh and less inclined to postpone them. For example, decision-making is difficult for me, so I take time in the morning to attend to that. If I find I have been putting off a task, I write it into my datebook to look at it first thing in the morning before I get involved in other tasks.

Being responsible and tending to "business" before we play is important. After we handle our responsibilities, we are better able to utilize our downtime to spark creative ideas. Typically, choosing recreation over responsibility leaves us feeling angry at ourselves, which is never conducive to the creative process. If you tend to be hard on yourself anyway, ignoring tasks that need attention will add one more layer of self-anger. I experience a feeling of exuberance once I complete that difficult chore. I know that if I wander into my painting studio with a host of unattended-to jobs, I usually cannot be completely present and open to ideas that otherwise may easily filter in. I may begin a painting, but then be preoccupied with what I "should be" doing.

Allow a good balance of work and play. This is particularly important for those of you who run your own businesses because every action and dollar is self-generated.

When we are responsible, we feel good; we feel free to use the balance of our time in ways that may be exciting creatively. Your dinner and a movie will be so much more fun without the "to-do list" milling around in the back of your mind.

15. Positive Vibes

Have you ever left a conversation or visit with someone feeling drained, angry, or depressed? Do you leave certain conversations with a feeling of inspiration? The energy fields and the personalities of others affect us, so carefully choose who you allow in. Of course, we cannot always control who we have to communicate with, but you can get creative in finding ways to gracefully limit your time with those who leave you feeling yucky. You may even discover ways of steering conversations away from the negative to spread more joy.

This key asks you to construct healthy boundaries. For many, this brings up feelings of guilt for being a "bad person" by not letting someone go on and on about their woes. But people who consider themselves perpetual victims deplete us; we need to steer clear of them. If you are in a situation where you don't have the luxury of completely eliminating negative interaction, such as at work, find ways to short-circuit conversations that are not constructive. If you try to point out the positive in a conversation with someone who is invested in being a victim, you will most likely be wasting your time and energy, so change the subject or find reasons to leave the conversation. For example, if you realize that so-and-so is going to continue their ranting about another person on the staff, you might chime in with: "I am sorry that you are having this problem with 'John,' but I really need to work on my deadline with _____. See you later." After a few times, the complainer will realize that you are not a satisfying audience for their negativity. They may also realize that you don't want to hear their complaints. The good news is that as you continue putting healthy boundaries in place, it becomes easier and easier to nip an annoying situation in the bud. Eventually, should you ever feel angry when you are confronted with one of these "victim" personalities, you will be able to disconnect without emotional drama.

When working, to make the most of your creative process, you need your best energy and that requires self-care. It may become necessary to let go of certain friends if they continue to cling to old, destructive behavior patterns that drain you. Letting go is never easy, but holding on to those who remain attached to destructive behavior patterns does not serve either of you. You will feel angry, and they will not have the opportunity to change if those around them allow them to continue as the victim.

Take inventory of the players in your life. Choose healthy relationships to ensure you have plenty of energy for your own creations.

16. Monitoring Your Energy

Being outdoors in nature, especially in the forest or at the ocean, contributes to a feeling of well-being for me. The smell of the pine in the forest makes me feel alive as does the salty sea air. Each day, I make sure to spend at least a few moments outdoors. Winter in the Northeast can be difficult for me because of the lack of sunlight and time to be outside.

Have you noticed that in certain places you find yourself feeling out of sorts? For example, take notice the next time you stay in a hotel or spend a few hours in a mall to see how the location influences your energy. Since I was a young girl, I can remember feeling depleted after a couple of hours in any mall. I still feel the same lack of energy in malls and experience the same thing at trade shows. Certain chemicals used in cleaning contribute to making some of us feel less than optimal. I don't do well with the recycled air. I know this about myself, so I make sure to go outdoors to take "deep breathing" breaks every so often. Take note of how your energy is after a couple of hours at your workplace to find out if you feel depleted. If you do, find ways to get a few moments of fresh air in order to stay healthy. How are you in crowds? Do you feel exhilarated by all the energies you are picking up from others? Or do you feel as if you need to run and hide?

With awareness, use some of the following suggestions to monitor your energy. Take a moment to close your eyes, tune in to your breath, and see if you are occasionally sighing (one of our bodies' ways of telling us we are tired), yawning, or if you are anxious. Examine whether you are feeling an urge for caffeine or sugar (another sign that your environment may be making you tired). Are you feeling inspired and thinking clearly?

Now that you are aware of what gives you good creative energy, make any needed adjustments to provide for that.

Call on your creativity to maximize your energy in any given situation. An essential-oil diffuser emitting a scent that you gravitate toward can go a long way toward making your environment more pleasing. If you must spend time in a less-than-ideal place, make sure to schedule a few breaks in refreshing atmospheres.

17. Visual Influence

The simple act of making a conscious decision to take a walk in nature instead of going to the gym (where you may be inundated with unsettling television sets featuring channels you don't want to watch) can make a difference in your mood, and that affects your productivity. Small changes like taking a moment in the morning to feel into your mood, or, on days when you find yourself less cheerful, choosing a different, more attractive route to work can make a big difference. Experiment with creating an intention to find inspiration and beauty, and see what pops up for you visually.

Are you aware of how what you are exposed to affects you? What we view may have more effect than we realize, and we don't always have control over our visual input. Becoming aware of the subtle ways in which our visual environment affects us can be useful in maintaining a peaceful state of being. The key is realizing whether the images you are exposed to contribute to or stifle your creativity.

There is an ongoing continuum between dreaming and the awakened state. What I see during the course of the day affects my dreams. If I have watched a violent television show or film, my dreams are almost always unsettling. In today's world, it can be difficult to escape the media. Even when we are in the airport a restaurant, a gym, or having an oil change for our car, we are bombarded with images and information that we may not wish to see. When I know that I may have a long wait, I prepare by bringing along reading material rather than become a captive audience to what is put in front of me in public places.

If you are having dinner with a friend in a bar, are you periodically paying attention to the television on the wall and not giving your friend full attention? Is the same thing happening in your home as you watch TV during mealtimes? This could be a prime time for catching up and staying connected to your spouse, family, or housemate. In our homes, we have more control. You many consider limiting your exposure to media at home in order to allow creative ideas to blossom in the fertile soil of peace and quiet.

When you do have control over your surroundings, become aware and selective about what you allow in. Within a month's time, you should see improvement reflected in your creative pursuits.

18. Repetitive Viewing

Visit the same scene at different times of the day as well as different times of the year. By viewing the same image at different times, we train our eyes (and ears if you like) to notice subtle changes. Become aware of subtle changes when the light hits your view on a different day or season. See how the light falling a certain way at a specific time sparks a memory like a romantic song or gives you a visual for a scene in a piece of your writing. Choose a scene, which can be indoors (as long as there is natural light) or outside. Be creative when selecting your setting.

I have practiced this key for years, first unintentionally and later intentionally when I suggested this as an assignment in my art classes. My students learn how to fine-tune vision by paying closer attention than they would normally. I enjoy hearing how amazed they are when they grow to view the world in a whole new way through this exercise.

If you are by nature a "visual type," someone who processes information by way of imagery, this will be easy and fun. If, however, you process in a more auditory or empathic manner, you may be able to exercise a new skill by building your visual awareness with this exercise. If you are a visual artist, I suggest that you take the exercise further by making a small, perhaps 5" x 7" sketch or painting of the scene each time you review it. (Note that this is a quick rendering; I don't recommend laboring over it.) Pay attention to the subtleties of how the image changes with the light. If you are not a visual artist, you may want to photograph your subject and later review the differences.

Take the time you need to make this exercise enjoyable. For example, you may pass by a particularly interesting tree while driving to work each day. Notice within a single day, or even within a couple of seasons, the differences in that tree. Watch the colors of the leaves change, then fall; note the shadows it casts in the morning and how they differ from later afternoon or even evening on the snow. If you choose to take your exercise further, learn to look for contrast by squinting your eyes. When you do this, you will notice that you can see the highlights of any given image as well as the darkest areas more easily. If you are painting or drawing the object, this will come in handy, and I suggest that you note these areas first in your piece of art, even just by marking lightly where these shapes land on your page. If you are not making a piece of art, you will still be training your eye to see with greater subtlety. You will be amazed at how your vision of the world as a whole changes. When my students first begin this exercise, they are thrilled with their new vision.

This key fine-tunes your creativity by sharpening your visual awareness. In making this exercise a habit, you will begin to repeat it in other situations automatically. The prime benefit of this key is learning to "see" in a new, expanded way. How wonderful!

19. Color Attraction

For a couple of years, I noticed that I was looking around my office with dissatisfaction. The cool yellow of my walls was bothering me. I was visualizing warm reds and golds and finally took the time out of my schedule to have it painted. Now when I enter the office I feel happy. The warm red is inviting and invigorating. Since this is an environment I spend lots of time in, it was well worth it to change the colors.

Your choice of color can also reveal what is going on for you emotionally. It's been proven that color has an effect on our state of mind. Therefore we can work with using color to feel good!

One way of experimenting with how you feel when surrounded by different colors is by noticing how you feel when walking into different colored rooms. Does it bring up fear when you walk into a red or black room? We often choose white or other light, subtle colors in decorating houses to make smaller rooms seem larger and to allow us to feel relaxed in the space. We may favor different colors at different points in our lives because of the effect that color has on our emotional selves. Purple is a color often related to spirituality; you will encounter it all over a New Age expo! I feel soothed when surrounded by lavender and have been known to paint entire apartments in varying shades accompanied by purple carpeting. Pink and blue both have soothing effects on me. I go through periods where I favor earth tones. Green in general tends to energize me. Purple is always a standby favorite.

Take notice of the colors that you resonate with and notice if they change. Awareness of how the colors you crave make you feel is an invitation to be bold and surround yourself with the energies that those colors contain. For example, if green is your calling, allow the freshness of this color to help conjure up new beginnings and healing in your life. If you find yourself drawn to pink, resonate love to yourself and others.

Have fun in your experiments with color. Paint your space in colors that inspire your creativity.

20. Enjoy the Creations of Others

I've been known to pull out a new canvas immediately upon coming home from a concert or dance performance. I'm notoriously inspired by both arts. Other visual artists also get me fired up to paint, so a trip to a museum or gallery can send me flying right into my studio. My inspirations don't always take form literally, although sometimes I will work from photos I take at a dance performance. The excitement of having seen or heard something that has touched a nerve is enough to make me want to go to work on my own piece of art. I have found myself inspired by listening to speakers and have taken note of their manner of speaking to implement in my own workshops.

Have you ever exited a concert, play, movie, or even someone's home and felt inspired to change something in your environment or create something new? This key encourages us to go out with eyes wide open as we move about our world, allowing the creations of others to spawn new ideas for us!

Do you spend enough time reviewing the creations of others? It's easy to stay caught up in our own routines and forget to switch things up to keep our viewpoints fresh and alive. Even if you are not working on a creative project, you will most likely find it easy to imagine getting excited about starting one after admiring someone else's creativity.

This could be just the right fuel for launching your own project.

Use this key to remind yourself to get out, enjoy, and get inspired by attending performances or concerts, exhibits, etc., to enhance your own projects.

21. Network

When I was in art school, one of my teachers advised us to go to as many art openings as we could and to make sure to meet at least one new person at every event. Because I tend to be shy, this was sometimes trying for me, but I decided to welcome the challenge. Your own networking does not need to be as specific as art openings, but getting out and about with others who share our interests can result in added creative spark. For example, if you are an avid or novice gardener, going on a garden tour can be very inspiring.

Surprises often await us when we are out and about. I have often left events with ideas springing up out of conversations that would not have occurred if I had stayed home. If you find it difficult to attend outings alone, invite a friend along to help you stick to the commitment to attend. If you tend to feel that you have nothing interesting to share, consider that your experiences differ from those you are conversing with; maybe sharing something that may seem mundane to you, such as how you collected and refinished a piece of furniture you gathered at a yard sale, may inspire another to explore their own treasure hunts.

Stay open to what may be places for catching and hatching creative ideas. By being aware of what's happening in your community or industry, you have an additional tool for keeping your stream of creative juices flowing. Enjoy your outings.

22. Judgment

Judgment of both ourselves and others can lead to creative shutdown. If we are too hard on ourselves, it becomes difficult to allow our creativity to flow in a free and healthy manner. If we are expending energy judging the work of others, we may be losing time that could be spent on our own creative endeavors. We may even become so intimidated by comparing ourselves to others that we stop the activity completely.

Examining why we have come to judge the fruits of our efforts harshly can be helpful. Perhaps we were given negative feedback from a teacher or another authority figure. If we have been criticized often, our own inner critic may emerge too often and we can miss the beauty of what we have created. I have been told repeatedly that I can't carry a tune, but loved ones enjoy hearing my squeaky voice singing "Happy Birthday" on their special day. When we are overcritical of our creations, we stand to miss what may be delightful to others. I witness this over and over in the art classes I teach. A student creates a wonderful painting during the course of a workshop but is so busy finding what is wrong with it that they miss the overall strength of the piece (that the rest of us are appreciating).

When you are working on a creation, you may have at least an idea of how it will be upon completion. It's always helpful to distance ourselves while we are working on the project to get an idea of where we are going with it. If we allow ourselves to become discouraged too early about what we have done, we may sabotage ourselves and lose our enthusiasm. When we aren't excited about our creations, it's difficult to complete the task.

It can be surprising how often we pass judgment. Have you ever noticed yourself judging the creations of your peers? If so, take a moment to contemplate why you may be doing that. Do you feel competitive with them? Are you worried that you are not doing a good enough job?

When we judge, we assume we are the one "in the know" and that we are superior in some way to the subject of our judgments. When we are busy judging the creations of others, the focus is off of our own creations, so there is less energy available to us.

If we are remarking negatively about someone else's creative project, are we feeling insecure about our own? Sometimes we criticize others because of our own insecurity. Noticing where we judge is an excellent guide for where *we* can shine our light. Get creative about how you can change habits of judging and turn the discoveries into ways of strengthening your own self-worth. When we put less focus on the other we have more energy for our own activities. If we find ourselves in a situation where we are asked our opinion and we may not be feeling positively about the subject of the inquiry, we can find creative, positive ways of expressing our opinions that will not be detrimental to anyone else.

The next time you find yourself in judgment of your own work, step back to examine whether you are jumping in too soon or if you are demanding too much from yourself. If you are judging another, check your motive for doing so. This key helps us to better accept self and others.

23. Accepting Advice

It's great to be open to feedback, but listening combined with a solid connection to our own ideas is necessary. It's also important to know *who* to go to, to be aware of their qualifications in an objective way. Sometimes staying true to our own wisdom is the best choice.

Using awareness combined with our creative faculties can assist us in deciding what is right. In my observation, folks generally fall into two categories here—those who assume that they are the best judges of any particular subject, and those who assume that others always know more than they do. Where do you fall? When we are listening without the barrier of our ego, we may find some useful feedback to weave into our creations.

Take notice of your response when you are offered advice. Do you tend to comment with something like, "Oh, I knew that already," or "That's obvious, why are you even saying that?" Or are you more likely to respond with something more along the lines of "Ah! How interesting! I never saw things from that perspective—thank you!" There are times when it's appropriate to receive feedback, but it's also important that we employ what feels to be best in our creative choices.

An awareness of how we receive information is helpful so that we can make the most of any valuable information that might be coming our way. If an expert in your field strongly dislikes a section of your painting or a chapter in your writing, will you automatically change it because you value this person's experience? Be objective about those you seek help from by reviewing their qualifications. I suggest being aware of your willingness to assume the other's judgment over your own when you are the creator of the undertaking.

Discernment also comes into play in our choices within our creative projects themselves. Do you have a tendency to stick with the tried and true or are you open to new ways of expression? Watch where you are accepting of ideas and methods you are familiar with instead of making way for new ones. It's good to be cognizant of what the reasons may be so you don't continue to get stuck in old behavior patterns.

The next time you prepare to ask for feedback, pause a moment to decide whether you do indeed need the opinion. If you proceed, pause again and reflect when you have gotten the response. This key will help you to know what is right for you.

24. Helping Out

Do you pay attention to the needs of people in your circle? When we are working on a project or have deadlines to meet, it's easy to become self-absorbed. We can get caught up in our own world and forget that others may need our attention. It's important to be available to those we care about or those to whom we can volunteer our time. Our willingness to serve can be a great springboard from which to discover new, creative ideas as we determine how to help.

In art school, I was told by a figure-drawing teacher that artists are the most selfish people in the world; they have to be. If you are an artist, whether amateur or professional, it takes a lot of time to create, and some mediums take more than others. I understand this too well, having had those around me clamoring for more attention. Family and friends need nurturing too—lots of it. Finding a balance is not always easy, but it's important.

Invoke your creative process here by exploring ways to make as much time as you can for others and still have the time you need for yourself. Giving back is important. Use your awareness to decide how much of yourself you can give and how best to do that. If you really don't have the time to donate, create other ways to give. It may be by way of financial contributions to causes close to your heart, or it can be as simple as gathering items around your home that you are not using, clothing that you have outgrown, and dropping it off at a shelter. Additionally, the nature of what you are creating may serve as your unique donation to the world.

What are you giving back? Find what is appropriate for you to give as your path of service, be it financial contribution or a gift of your time, love, or talent. Let this key serve as a reminder to you to make it a habit to step back from what you are caught up in and donate time, love, or talent to a person or group of your choosing.

25. Speak Up!

Expressing emotions can be difficult. If you stifle your resentments and bite your tongue in order to avoid confrontation you are not only disrupting your flow of creativity, you are doing a disservice for all involved. The first step is recognizing the situations that make speaking up so hard. Let's look at how you can treat these situations as invitations to explore how you might successfully get your message across.

If someone has made a remark that is hurtful to you, letting them politely know gives you a feeling of empowerment and may enlighten your friend, who may not have realized that they have struck a nerve. This serves both of you while decreasing the chances of a similar event happening again. Plus, you will walk away feeling good about having expressed yourself.

In most cases, we don't speak up because of fear. How many times have you not realized until after the conversation that you were not okay with a remark or action because you were so surprised at it? When we are present, and therefore aware, we recognize right away when we may have been adversely affected or when we ourselves may have said or done something inappropriate. If you have said or done something that does not feel right, or may have been hurtful or inaccurate, be strong enough to own your actions and apologize. If you are afraid to apologize, call in your awareness to discover why. It's helpful to trace the root of our fears so that we may move through them more easily with practice. In making ourselves vulnerable, we actually become stronger by speaking our truth. If you feel that your apology will be dismissed, find a way to say it with love and let go of expectations of how the other person will react. By doing this you will have done the best you can.

Perhaps you feel you deserve a raise at work. Are you afraid to ask? Can you identify why you are afraid? After you have recognized your fear, get creative to find ways of asking for what you want.

Use this key to become aware of when you are feeling afraid and move through those fears to be a stronger *you*. We can find the courage to face our fears. Put yourself in places where you know you can blossom and speak up!

26. Listen to Your Body

Many of us are so wrapped up in our daily activities that we are unaware of when we are tired or hungry. To maintain a positive mindset and good physical health, we must make our physical needs a priority. We can be creative in deciding how to best maintain optimum health, but no matter what is done, bear in mind that the connection between the body and mind is critical.

How do you maintain your connection to your body? It may be helpful to keep a diary. Notice the days that you are particularly productive and think about it. What did you eat that day—as well as the day before? Did you get a good night's rest? Was your activity level higher or lower than normal? Your body needs a certain amount of physical exercise. Of course everyone's system is different. I tend toward poor circulation; if I don't get enough movement during a day, I feel sluggish that evening as well as the next day, and it eventually takes a toll.

Have you noticed that on a day when you have not gotten enough sleep or when you have eaten or drunk too much the night before you may be sluggish when you show up to the drawing table, work bench, or office? Checking in before you order dessert or that last glass of wine to see if your body can handle it can go a long way toward maintaining optimum creativity. I like to pause and consider the future effects of the decision. If I am tired due to an extra drink, I am not inclined to make it a good workday.

In addition to listening, you need to be able to respond to your body's needs, so plan ahead to provide some optimum energy resources. Try boiling up a dozen eggs as a handy portable protein boost. The next time you are shopping, keep in mind nutritional foods or healthy food bars that can be carried along with you for easy energy sources. Take some time on your day off to create healthy meals that can be made serving size and frozen so that you have yummy and healthy meal options.

In terms of exercise, how can we get our bodies to move? Maybe your body automatically starts to sway when you hear music. Or you may respond well to the amazing balance of body and mind that both yoga and the martial arts provide. Some of you may love the endorphin rush following running and swimming. If the thought of any of the above is undesirable, you may find fulfillment by way of a walk in nature.

Do more of what works for you; make a commitment to staying on track with that to help encourage your creative efforts. Remember that if your body is healthy, you will have more of a drive to take your creative powers to their heights!

27. Take a Break

Are you aware of the formula for how *you* are most productive? Some folks find it more difficult to focus than others and may need to take more breaks or find ways to discipline themselves by creating and committing to a schedule. Where do you fall here? If you are writing and find your mind wandering, then maybe it's time to get up and do some laundry or make lunch—anything to switch up the energy.

Working hard is not always the best choice for feeding the soul. Sometimes being disciplined does *not* pay off. When we are working on a project with the proverbial "nose to the grindstone," we may get caught up in the details and lose sight of the big picture. Take breaks in order to return to the focus of your concentration with new eyes, ears, or thoughts.

I might even choose to take a break within an activity. For example, if I am working on a painting and cannot figure out how to make a particular section look good, I will switch to a different canvas and when I return to the first one I can see it with fresh eyes and know exactly how to solve the problem.

I'm someone who needs physical activity on a daily basis in order to feel good, so I often get started on my project and arrange my day so that my break involves something physical. Most of the time I return with more energy, but that's just me. I know writers who get up in the middle of the night to write and easily fall back asleep. Some of us forget to eat when we are working on creative projects. Are you aware of when you need some recharging? Giving our bodies the fuel they need is important for optimal creativity.

An awareness of how you function for best productivity is the challenge. Remember to honor the ways in which you as an individual work best by giving yourself what *you* need to rejuvenate.

28. Fuel

We want our bodies to be functioning at optimal levels in order to be productive. If we are sluggish and low in energy, it may be due to how we are fueling our physical vehicles. Begin by taking note of how you feel physically, right now, in this moment. Do you have optimal energy or do you want to reach for that cup of coffee or candy bar to give you a boost? Is your mind fuzzy? Have you been eating well or eating on the run? Are you taking in large amounts of caffeine and/or sugar to give you energy? If so, this is a sign that your nutrition needs attention.

Due to factors such as chemical additives, GMOs, and even pollution in our water, air, and the earth itself, receiving appropriate nutrition can be difficult. Conflicting information from the media, along with dietary trends (that often promote inconsistent recommendations) coming and going all the time, constantly adds to the confusion to the point that we may lose touch with what our body actually needs. In these hectic times when people are working more hours and life seems to be busier than ever for many, it's important to use your creativity to find healthy ways to fuel up.

Some people think healthy eating takes too much time and effort, but employing your creativity to make dietary changes can be very satisfying. Monitor how these changes affect you and choose menus that work easily into your lifestyle. If you get up very early and are in the habit of skipping breakfast or eating on the run, it could well be worth your while to invest in either a juicer or a powerful blender. Purchasing high-quality protein powder from a health food store to add to smoothies can provide excellent supplements for maximum nourishment. Getting the proper nutritional supplements based on what your individual body needs is helpful. According to sources such as the Cornucopia Institute, in the past we were able to get our vitamins and minerals from the foods we eat, but because of pollution and soil depletion most of us need additional supplements.

Of course, determining the precise amount of vitamins and minerals for optimal performance is daunting—and near impossible—so here is a simple experiment to conduct to demostrate the dramatic impact food can have on your well-being. Just try eliminating one known problematic food such as sugar for at least a couple of weeks to see if you notice changes in your mood and what you accomplish. (My guess is that you will notice positive results).

When we feel good physically, we are more alive, more present, and more ready to receive and act upon the next great idea! Use this as a reminder to make the effort to take good care of your body.

29. Location Inspiration

Have you noticed that you may feel different in various geographical locations? Did you feel like you were "home" the first time you visited an area you ended up moving to? Or perhaps a different section of the country or another country feels like another planet. We may come up with fresh ideas when in a new environment. Landscape painters are inspired by the look of different locales—in terms of differences in trees, flowers, and wildlife. Writers are known to retreat to or research areas they choose to write about, and musicians are certainly aware of different sounds in new surroundings. My own creativity is greatly influenced when I travel. I've noticed that different architectures, cultures, and new natural surroundings inspire me and instantly make me want to paint.

+ If you have not traveled out of the area where you were brought up, you can still use your awareness to discover what may fuel you in another location. You have probably seen places on television or in a movie that looked intriguing. Take stock of your memories of places you have visited. What is it that surfaces for you in these memories? Are there any particular sensations?

Contemplate the following:

+ Imagine any places you would like to visit. What is your pull toward these places?

+ Do you long to visit New York or Hong Kong and be stimulated by bustling crowds? Or perhaps you yearn to visit the dry, empty desert—could this indicate that you are craving more space? Or are they by the ocean or a lake—perhaps bringing you feelings of expansion from the water?

Use this key to extract the ingredients of places that inspire you and find ways to creatively implement ideas based on these—such as decorating a room in a southwestern theme. Let your imagination run with these ideas!

30. Cultural Diversity

I always pack my watercolors when I visit someplace new. One of the reasons I began using small portable paints instead of oils was so that I could easily document my travels. I've painted at sacred sites in Mexico, Bali, the British Isles, Malta, and Greece. I was called to visit Morocco because I found myself fascinated by the beautiful architecture, especially the numerous arches that abound. I made a trip there and was visually rewarded far beyond what I could have imagined. The buildings, the desert, the winding paths through the markets as well as the colorful towers of spices thrilled me. As usual, I did a few paintings on the spot. I also took lots of photos and have since referred to them as content in many paintings, including some of my most popular images.

Visiting other cultures provides valuable teachings. If you are fortunate enough to do this in real life, go for it! You may alternately experiment with reading or reviewing documentaries about other cultures to see if they ignite any creative sparks.

Although I primarily create through a visual medium, the sounds and smells of the places I visit also stir my soul. I was with a friend who recorded a heartbeat from the ancient Goddess temples in Malta by leaving her recorder sitting on the stones! She was also moved to write some amazing new song material while sitting out among the sacred sites in England, allowing the presence of the mighty stones and ancient wells to be transformed into beautiful new melodies.

Have you noticed any particular cultures that attract you? You may choose to investigate some of their music, clothing, or décor for inspiration. Even if you don't actually travel to these locations, the wealth of the histories of these cultures may hold delicious bases or accents for your creative efforts.

Take notice of what cultures beckon to you and see how you might find material there that you can integrate into your projects. Open up to new ways of experiencing the diverse and colorful cultures that are a part of our wonderful planet.

31. Fun with Children

Children will grab anything and turn it into the most fantastic of objects. They don't need expensive or elaborate toys. In fact, perhaps they may be better off without them because it gives their already-vivid imaginations more chance to stretch. That's why being around children can help us experience renewed creative inspiration. Have you observed children at play? Kids often see and hear things that we don't sense at all. Some of that may be because they are making it up, or it may be that they are closer to the Spirit realm when very young. Children are said to be able to see fairies, angels, and the like—an ability we seem to lose with age.

When I grew up, there were far fewer toys and no internet. Therefore, a lot of my recreation involved using whatever was at hand and letting my imagination run wild. One memory that stands out, for some odd reason, is one of myself and a friend taking a stick and a slice of white bread and turning it over and over, imagining that we were roasting it over a fire. We were convinced we saw it turn brown and knew when it was ready!

Obviously types of activities vary between the sexes but both girls and boys take such joy in certain games of interest. For me many activities took place out of doors in the forest, so there were usually tree forts continually being constructed, then improved upon. I used to go outside for jaunts where I set intention to hunt for things, especially of the creature variety such as butterflies, turtles, and the like.

Make the time to spend with children because their bubbly, spontaneous energy can be contagious. Drink from the fountain of youth and spread the energy to your own creative projects.

32. Choices

I can't tell you how many folks I encounter who inform me that they have a book they want to write or that they once were an artist and want to go back to it "someday." I also have folks tell me they want to take one of my workshops "someday." I am often tempted to ask when "someday" is … I believe that if we really want to do something, we make it happen unless there are logistical reasons beyond our control. One of those logistical reasons is usually money, and if you really think about the worst possible finanacial scenario, it's not an insurmountable challenge. Some lifestyle changes will need to happen, but many folks will find that we have enough freedoms in our lives that we can make some, if not all, of the choices to bring about the things that are important to us.

Have you spent a lot of time going back and forth over a choice connected to what or how to use your creativity? The inability to make a decision because you feel overwhelmed is an easy excuse for not showing up and creating, but the solution is simple: Make dates to create and show up.

Consider your priorities. What is it that you choose to create in this lifetime of yours? If there is something that is on your "someday list," I encourage you to consider how badly you want this. If the decision is that you indeed do want to do this, I suggest figuring out some initial steps to move forward. If you are clear about your desire and are ready to begin, make some monthly, weekly, and daily choices to take action. This could include doing research, taking classes, or simply making some initial calls.

It's possible that subconsciously you may not really plan to move ahead with this desire. I suggest getting very quiet within yourself to discover whether you do indeed choose to follow the yearning you have. We can get so used to saying something repeatedly that we may not realize that it is not a current wish. Letting "it" go if it is not something that you are willing to totally commit to is healthy. It will free you to find what you *really* want.

Choosing to follow or change your pursuit can bring you a feeling of empowerment. Your choices reflect the essence of who you are, and when you commit to them you will blossom.

33. Commitment

In our culture, creativity is not usually at the top of the list of priorities. Creativity needs nurturing in order to sustain itself. It feeds off of itself. With commitment, we take action on an idea and see how opening the door to a new creative project can lead to the next idea. Even at this stage of the game, I find myself needing to actually schedule painting time into my calendar. I usually make sure to take at least a month, which may be split up, for my own creations outside of the work I do for others or for my business. If I don't, I find myself answering to what needs to be done for my business—and miss opportunities to paint, which make for a cranky Melissa!

Are you aware of what might prevent you from showing up for your creative endeavors? Most artists I've known (and that's a lot) find that they are either too busy or they just procrastinate when it comes to finding the time for their own projects. Anything else such as work, socializing, tending to the needs of others, can end up taking priority. What does it take for *you* to show up on a regular basis? Do you plan ahead and stick to your project dates? One gift that comes as a result of committing and showing up is that you may discover that the more time you spend with what you are creating, the easier it is to return to it. I suggest that you commit to specific times that you will spend with your creative pursuits.

Call upon and stick to your intention in this key by making a commitment to your creativity and showing up at the designated times. Enjoy the feeling of fulfillment that comes from honoring your commitments.

INTUITIVE OR HEART-BASED KEYS:

Allow Your Inner Compass
To Guide You.

At some point in our lives, most of us come upon a situation where we just can't seem to make a move because we are not sure which path to take. Perhaps you are miserable at your job and want to leave but don't know if the timing is right or if you will find something else that is a better fit. Or maybe you are considering ending a relationship because you are just not sure if he or she is "it." We all possess an inner "knowing" as to which path to choose but we often don't trust it.

My goal in writing this section is to help you become acquainted with how you can best use your inner compass to help guide your way. Our intuition is a powerful tool that we can engage on a regular basis. Perhaps you are aware of an instance in your life when you ignored a "gut" feeling. Have you found yourself in that "if I had it all to do again…" conversation? Whenever I have ignored my instincts, I have regretted it. On the other hand, I cannot recall regretting any times that I *have* listened. Using your intuition can help you navigate the potholes of life and also serve as an additional tool for help in your creative process.

Everyone is intuitive. When I present exercises in the classes I teach on psychic development, almost everyone is shocked to discover just how intuitive they really are. Intuition speaks to me from my solar plexus (the area about two fingers above the bellybutton). If I have a yes to something, I feel as if I want to physically move in a forward direction. If I receive a no, I feel as if I am shrinking backward. If I don't listen to my intuitive guidance, I sometimes experience a slight sense of dread, sometimes a slight feeling of guilt. I know that I am being spoken to from my core, and in not listening I am betraying myself. Other people I know experience sadness or fear when they don't listen to their inner guidance. Are you aware of how you feel when you ignore your inner voice?

If you don't see yourself as intuitive, consider that we learn to engage this part of ourselves when we are children. As kids, when those around us smile we realize we have behaved well and we receive attention or praise. With intuition, we learn how to relate to those who raised us by understanding when the best times are to ask for what we want, or maybe when we can get away with something we are forbidden to do. We also understood what to do to gain the approval of our authority figures or friends.

If you look back on your childhood you can gain insights into where you were heading even at that young age. I was a student of Barbara Brennan, the well-known energy healer, and she taught us in our energy-healing classes that the games or activities we were engaged in as children are most likely reflected in our current lives. We *knew* where we were heading! I used to create "plays" (mini theater productions) and function as the director. When I am posing folks for paintings, I am reminded of how familiar and comfortable that role is for me. I also used to collect rock specimens; I had boxes and boxes of them, besides saving the ones I picked up from the ground. Currently my love for stones is reflected in my collection of healing crystals.

We dream every night. Our dreams can become a significant tool for working with our intuitive faculties because using our intuition is helpful in understanding our dreams. Dreams enrich our lives by adding color and magic. The day after I have a significant dream, I enjoy ruminating on it, accepting the challenging of exploring how it relates to my current life. It's a bit like doing a jigsaw puzzle. Allow your dreams to become a powerful means for accelerating or fine-tuning your intuitive skills.

The key exercises in this section can be a lot of fun. I love sending messages telepathically and waiting to see if they are received. I do this on a daily basis—even with my cats—and am amazed (though I shouldn't be) when I "call" one of them to come upstairs to my bed and next thing I know there's a warm fuzzy body lying next to me. I'm sure you have had instances where you called someone only to hear them exclaim that they had just been thinking of connecting with you. Pay attention to any twinges and spurts of energy in your body that may be relaying a message. Listen with a sensitive ear. Take the risk of functioning as often as possible from your *inner* knowing.

Our intuition is invaluable in the creative process. When we are tuned in, we are open to discover sources of inspiration. We are guided to advisors, teachers, and fellow collaborators. For example, if you are working on a campaign at your job and you have an urge to contact a specific client, *go for it*! Your intuition is speaking! If you feel the urge to sit with someone in particular over lunch, perhaps you will be rewarded with an idea the two of you came up with while chatting. Also, we will have greater trust in our decisions regarding our creative projects such as knowing when a work is complete.

The keys I detail in this section will take some time and focus but will serve as distinct barometers for you to observe, as your intuitive capabilities grow stronger. Just as in the other two categories of keys, we will be able to fine-tune our intuition to enhance our ability to create by using these ideas. This handy inner compass is available to us at all times. Let's get going and practice how to sharpen our intuition for ongoing creative success.

34. Tune In!

Have you ever deliberately focused your mind on an individual to determine what's up with them, where they are, or how they might be feeling? Perhaps you had not heard from an old friend in some time and wondered if they were okay, or maybe you had a date with someone and wondered if they reciprocated your enthusiasm?

Even if we have not been consciously aware we were doing it, each of us has "tuned in" to someone or something else. If we think about a person, we might naturally be able to tune in and we may see an image of that person, hear a phrase, or feel a sensation in our own physical body. If we understand *how* this information relates to that person or situation, we have a better chance of excellent communication with them. Tuning in is a deliberate act. It requires action on our part.

How can you tune in? It varies to some degree for each of us. My way is to become very still, go inside, and open to imagine the subject or issue of my query. To "go inside" means to shut out the outside world in order to be completely available to receive any incoming information. I allow what wants to show itself when I am in my still space. I may receive what shows itself visually or through my inner hearing. When I am doing this ideally I am alone and seated in a quiet place where I know I will not be disturbed. I have my eyes closed to tune out the external world. I have voiced my inquiry either silently or out loud.

I practice tuning in often because of the many intuitive readings I do. Because I tend to be primarily visually oriented, the most natural method for me is to either look at a picture or simply imagine an image if I am familiar with the subject. I take my time and wait to receive my information, staying quiet until something surfaces, be it by way of an image or a message in a sentence or phrase. I often receive very specific details that may not relate to a person's query but these details let me know that I am on the right "channel," that I am absolutely connecting with their being. I've even gotten responses by way of songs! I tune in after asking my question either silently or out loud and can easily receive some return information by way of a visual image in my mind, or by an internal "hearing." My own capacities for receiving information by tuning in have continued to strengthen and shift over the years. As you develop your skills know that regardless of how you tune in, your *deliberate focus* on your desired subject is the key to achieving results from this exercise.

Strengthening your intuition can be accomplished but requires steady practice even if you are already a natural. Enjoy enhanced intuitive capacities by creatively practicing tuning in with stillness, focus, and awareness.

35. Deep Listening

Spirit speaks in many ways! *Be aware* to help ensure you don't miss any messages. Practicing being present (as we discussed in key 12) in each moment will help you to avoid missing possible clues. Listening not only means hearing in the traditional sense—we may also hear things in our "inner ear" almost like a small voice or whisper. We might find guidance in a single line of a reading or single spoken sentence giving helpful clues to a completely different issue or topic. I may pick up ideas while conversing with friends that I can implement in writing, painting, or teaching. Those ideas come simply from paying attention to how differently someone else perceives the topic of our discussion.

When listening to Spirit we need to be as objective as possible when we take in information. If we are invested in or are entangled by our own views of the subject, it can be difficult to take in what the other person is presenting. In cases such as this, I let go of any need to be an authority or "right" so that I can have a solid understanding of the other person's point of view.

In some situations, we have more freedom than in others in terms of how we are listening. I find it fascinating how I can present a poem or song at a workshop for students to paint about, and how differently the various participants perceive the gist of the material. For one student the poem may feel sad, but to another it could evoke a beautiful but slightly melancholy feeling, while others may read something completely different into it. Calling on our intuition gives us a better understanding of what is meant to be conveyed and where it fits. If we can also "listen" for a *feeling* while we receive information, we may grasp the subtle meaning of what is communicated. Paying attention to body language can also be a powerful form of listening.

Intuition comes in handy when we are seeking help from the Divine. Have you ever asked a question and soon after had a visitation in nature, such as a butterfly crossing your path, finding a feather at your feet, seeing a flock of wild turkeys running in front of you? Even though your message comes in visually, it still requires "listening" on your part because it is a visual response to a question you asked. How do you interpret this magical response from nature? You will need to listen to your gut instinct. I love these messages, for they are reminders that I am being watched over.

Make the practice of calling upon your intuition to fine-tune your listening skills a fun challenge. Your enhanced ability to know what works for you will guide you in your creative projects.

36. Be Receptive

We receive "incoming" all day long: information, emotions, physical objects, weather, sounds, smells, and so on. What have you received so far today? Perhaps you detected a shift in the weather as you opened your door for the first time. How did that feel? Could the beauty and freshness of a spring day give you inspiration? Did you open the door to three feet of snow, instantly setting off a feeling of despair that you could call upon to express in the poem or novel you are writing? Perhaps your day began with a phone call from an old friend that prompted joyous or crazy memories—more fuel for creativity!

Receiving is both an active and a passive state. Making the choice to be receptive is the active part of that equation. By invoking our creativity, we open ourselves to different ways of interpreting what we have received as well as gain new material for our creative projects. In order to actually receive the information, we let go into a more passive state. We can enter a passive state by becoming very quiet and letting our thoughts drift away. With no thoughts to focus on, we are relaxed and at the "still point," a place of neutrality where new information can find its way in if we choose to allow it. Learning to meditate is the most direct way to get familiar with finding your way into this passive/receptive state of being.

Sometimes our intuition gives us important clues about what is going on with those in our lives. If you have a hunch to call someone when you receive a thought or feeling about them, do you act on it for confirmation? Sometimes we take these "incoming spurts" for granted without realizing that we are receiving what could be important information. I can be anywhere, anytime and have what I call a "flash" about someone. I learned to make note of these and casually check in to see if I am on target. Nine times out of ten, there is at least some sort of correlation between the content of the "flash" and what is currently going on with that person.

Your intuition gets a good workout when you actively practice receiving. Employ creative thinking when you get your bits and pieces of information to see how they might fit together, especially in relation to creative projects you are pursuing.

37. Send

Have you ever tried sending a friend a psychic message? Can you remember a time when you thought of someone who immediately contacted you? Or vice versa—you called someone and they let you know that they had just written to you. Who was the sender and who was the receiver?

Find a willing partner and try the following experiment:

1. Decide which of you will be the sender and which will be the receiver.

2. Choose a convenient time and agree that one of you will send a message to the other.

3. Decide in what way the sender will launch the message. It might be through:

    a. A strong visual picture.

b. Playing a song and concentrating
on the melody or the lyrics.

c. Releasing an odor from cutting
open a lemon or spraying a fragrance.

4. Test your results. You should also try
alternating the methods of sending via
the senses before the two of you switch roles.

The gifts here are twofold. You will discover whether you are a better sender or receiver as well as *how* you send and receive easiest.

Here are some additional experiments:

+ If you are taking a class, send the teacher a message
to call on you when everyone's hand is raised.

+ Send a message to a friend you have not
spoken to in ages and notice how long it
takes to get a response, if at all.

+ Silently call your pet to visit you and
notice how long it is before they appear.

Don't get discouraged if your recipients don't respond. Just as we have better literal communication with some folks, we connect with some people's energetic vibrations more easily as well. And it could be as simple as your recipient feeling under the weather and not receiving from you when they might have at another time.

Many of us engage in prayer. The effects from the power of sending love and prayers have been well documented. Prayers are a daily ritual for me; I begin and end the day by sending love and prayers to those in need and whoever else comes to mind.

With send, we find an excellent arena for blending our intuition and creativity because we can call upon our imagination to create an *infinite* number of ways to use and therefore strengthen our intuition.

38. Contemplation

Do you have something that you have already identified that you may want to explore creatively? Contemplation of why this is intriguing to you can be helpful because understanding *why* you are called to this activity will accentuate these aspects in your creations. As you contemplate, notice if your attraction is aesthetic, emotional, intellectual, or otherwise appealing to you. Just *what is it* about this "thing" that calls to you? For example, if I am going through a batch of photos to choose something to paint, I narrow down my choices and spread them out in front of me. When I make my final choice,

I take a good look and consider why this photo interests me. If I understand that for me it is the mood of that image that is drawing my attention, I may make color, medium, or size choices that will emphasize that mood.

Perhaps you enjoy fabrics; contemplate how you can make the best of that fondness. In doing so, you may choose to learn to make a quilt or decide to sew some intricate new curtains. If you are somewhat of a foodie, you may consider what some of your favorite taste combinations are and experiment with some new culinary creations.

When we pause and take a detached look at things, we are able to be objective, thus allowing the realization of creative ideas that may be resting in the background. Contemplation differs from meditation in that *contemplation* infers a subject—"What are we contemplating about?"—whereas the word *meditation* suggests going into the still point, the place of no thinking at all. We can use contemplation to unearth hidden treasures for creative focus.

If you have not received your creative "calling," reflect upon what has been recently showing up to inspire you. Use your intuition to feel into what may be lurking in your subconscious, or perhaps showing up repeatedly in your surroundings. Once you have identified what may be "up" for you, I suggest stepping back and examining why this element is appearing.

Contemplation helps you to become familiar with how you can identify undiscovered interests or refine existing ones. Follow your discovery by jumping in with an expanded awareness of how to make the most of your creativity.

39. Dream Work

Dreams are a wild and wonderful resource for understanding our inner workings. Learning what our soul (or unconscious, subconscious, angels, or guides) is trying to tell us in dreamtime can often require us to use our imagination in a very broad way. Literal interpretation of dreams is not as beneficial as looking at them more metaphorically.

Immediately upon waking from a dream, I review it as objectively as possible. While I am still in a semi-conscious state, I am more easily able to come to an understanding of the meaning of my dream. I call upon my intuition to gain understanding of any messages by looking at the dream from a detached point of view, as an observer. Often my dreams are a direct reflection of activities and issues happening in my life at the time, bringing me a greater awareness of my emotional state of being.

Carl Jung was a Swiss psychiatrist who taught that there are archetypical themes in dreams that cross over from culture to culture with specific meanings. He noted certain dream symbols that possess the same universal meaning for all men and women. He terms this phenomenon the "collective unconscious." I subscribe to that idea, and I also feel that because dreams are personal—we must imprint our own individual meanings within each one. Others teach that the different characters in the dreams are all different aspects of ourselves. I try out all of these in my detective work for meaning in my dreams.

Dream Themes

To title dreams helps to understand them—by titling we are forced to consider the theme of the dream. Sometimes it works to try and figure out the images and situations intellectually, but if we can't do that rationally, we can instead acknowledge what emotion might have been attached to that dream. If I have a dream that is very upsetting, I may find that it directs me to an area of unfinished business. For example, I may wake to memories of fun times with an old friend that I have had a falling out with and the dream might help me to come to a decision about whether I want to repair the friendship or let it go.

Working with Dreamtime Information

I believe that Spirit and my guides help me during my dreamtime. I call these "teaching dreams," and those dreams can leave me exhausted upon waking. I've had memories of being in ceremony with powerful teachers, and even if I wake up tired, I feel grateful because I know a special teaching has taken place. These dreams are different because they have a special, very powerful sensation and they are rare.

In some indigenous cultures dreams are taken very seriously. In the morning, the first thing the tribe does is share their dreams and consider the gifts from dreams as a form of information, such as where to move next or what may happen with the weather.

Getting the Maximum Benefits from Your Dreams

Each night before I go to sleep, I speak out loud and ask Spirit and my guides for help during dreamtime. If I have a particular issue that I need help with, I state that as well. Usually dreams that I remember that follow this practice are connected to the issue.

Writing down our dreams helps us to remember them. We can also come to a better understanding of our dreams by sharing them. Others often see things that we may miss. Whether you are doing an exchange or solo review, the sooner upon waking that you examine your dreams, the easier it is to grasp their meaning.

Discover and learn to interpret the gifts in your dreams to maximize the benefits of these subconscious offerings. You will get a creative workout by learning to wrap your mind around the colorful scenarios that go on every night!

40. Be Flexible

I can get very fixed in my thinking at times. Making art reminds me to think outside of the "box" and is my method of moving into solving a problem. I can accomplish this on canvas by way of ideas that would not normally enter my mind. I may think that I need to have a wolf in a painting but I am flexible enough to accept that if the composition I have created does not accommodate the size or color of a wolf, I need to be willing to accept that and let the painting's initial theme evolve. It's so easy to get stuck with our original impetus for a creation. I find it exciting to experiment with choices other than my initial idea to discover how a concept can expand in different directions.

Being flexible is a major key to expanding creativity. All of the arts are great teachers of change. Many times my students come to class determined to paint a particular theme. However, the paintings themselves may dictate the next stroke and even a change in theme. Cultivating flexibility is a tool to use in all areas of our lives to bring us more joy. When we let go of what we think we wanted, the release into what's next can be very liberating.

Our intuition is helpful in knowing where we need to be flexible and how we can do that. For example, in planning your weekend (or any other time you may have off), use your intuition to decide when you may best accomplish the mandatory chores and be creative in scheduling the rest of your activities to your satisfaction. I may intuit that I will want to paint during the day, so I work the rest of my activities around that, using my best energy for my art and working the other errands and chores to give that priority.

Flexibility, within the scope of any creative endeavor, opens the way to an ongoing ability to open up to new and different ways of seeing things that carry over from creative projects to every aspect of daily living. Use this information to enjoy a greater flexibility in *all* areas of your life.

41. Ask/Listen

Have you found yourself asking Spirit for guidance on a situation and found yourself watching for "signs" that may be your answer? The simple act of asking a question and paying attention to whatever messages come through in whatever variety of ways can become second nature. I find reward in reading the responses in nature. There are numerous stories of folks feeling that they communicated via butterflies with loved ones that have passed away. Because I paint so many butterflies, people often write and share the most magical stories about how these beautiful winged creatures have appeared to signal all sorts of messages, but most of them have to do with deceased loved ones who wanted to let them know that they are still around and accessible.

A silly game I have played with myself since my teen years is to ask a question, then turn on the radio to see what surfaces as the first song or just switch the station and discover a song that speaks to that query. I then use my intuition to help understand the clues. Though this is not my most valid method of listening, I find it fun and a good intuitive exercise because it helps me open my mind to creative interpretation.

I have made it a practice to ask Spirit and my guides for help with an issue before I go to sleep to see what may surface in my dreams, but I don't limit this activity to dreamtime.

If I am lost, I can simply walk down the street and ask for signs to lead me in the right direction. I may also use that walk as an opportunity to ponder a situation that I need help with and find signs that represent solutions. I almost always receive direction; I just need to know how to interpret what I am being sent.

A common misstep with this exercise is being too literal with interpretations of what might appear as "signs." Here is where intuition comes in handy: after you have put out your question (whether internally or externally voicing it), let go of your rational, analytic mind and relax into a more receptive consciousness. Be open to *all* of your senses. If you are visually oriented, you may likely obtain your answer in images. If you are more of an auditory type, you may be inclined to hear your message. If you are empathic, you may receive the message by way of a sensation within your body. I am empathic so I am accustomed to the sensations I feel when I am tuned in. They are sometimes very subtle, but they are definitely there. For example, when I am doing a reading for someone and I have a sensation such as a short very slight pain or a quick twitch in a part of my body, this tells me that the client has something to explore in that same physical location in their own body.

The ask-listen technique can help you learn how *you* are most likely to receive your information. And it's fun! You'll delight in the insights that you may previously have been inclined to miss.

42. Honor Your Hunches

We don't always know why we "get a feeling" about something, but if we honor our hunches we are likely to be rewarded. For example, if we let our intuition direct us to our next piece of reading material, we may be surprised by what we find. As creatives, when we practice following what attracts us without overanalyzing, we are exercising our creative muscles.

Honoring one's hunches requires trust. I've never regretted honoring my hunches, but I *have* regretted *not* listening to them. Can you recall a decision you made that went against your inner grain? I surely can. During those times, it can be helpful to look at why we made decisions that were not in alignment with what we felt would be best. By taking an honest look at why we chose not to follow our inner voice we can discover keys to why we carry old patterns of self-doubt, allowing us opportunities to replace these inner messages or fears with a stronger, more confident sense of self.

To work with this key, get creative about following small "cues" you receive during the day. If you are driving and get an urge to take a different route, don't question it, act on it. If you have a notion to call someone, get on the phone! Take this as an invitation to discover the benefits of acting on your hunches to see what may transpire.

43. Social Intuiting

Social situations like parties or other gatherings with strangers are great arenas to practice honing your intuitive skills. Here is a fun exercise: simply notice who you are drawn to, without asking yourself why you feel pulled. As you discreetly gaze at this person, allow the brain to go "soft" and notice what impressions you receive. For example, you might question whether the person is married, has kids, where they live, and more. Later on during the gathering, try to find an opportunity to speak with that person or, if you miss that chance, ask someone who knows them if what you perceived about them was accurate.

You can also find other ways to use a social situation for intuiting. When you first arrive at a social function (and you don't know most of the people), scan the room quickly and, without putting too much thought into it, see if you can predict who will be the life of the party, who will sit on the sidelines, whom you may end up conversing with, or who will connect with whom. You might also see if you can intuit what time the event will have its high point and when it will be over. You don't need to limit this challenge to party situations. You can watch a movie, focus on one of the actors that you like and do the same thing. (You can confirm your hunches about the movie, the actor in question, and more with some internet research—after, not during, the movie.)

If you want to ramp it up a bit, try tuning in to the event before you go. You can decide to focus on a general mood of the event, who may attend, what might be served, or any of the above mentioned questions that you will be able to confirm after arrival.

Social intuiting can make gatherings more interesting, especially if you do not feeling like attending. Be sure to make the most of your upcoming activities by creatively testing out your abilities.

44. Let's Pretend

Why *not* dream big? Our fantasies create our realities! Yes they do! Even if you do not attain your total fantasy, you may be content to move further in that direction. If you are unhappy at your job and pretend you are at your perfect job, you may discover the elements of what you would like in a work environment, allowing you to search for that when you are ready to take action to make a career change.

It's very helpful to be able to "see it" to help make "it" happen, whatever "it" is for you. Limited thinking stands in the way of imagining what we can create. I also find it helpful to discuss what I want to create to affirm it, which makes it more real and brings things into sharper focus.

I've played "let's pretend" by way of fantasizing for as long as I can remember. It's not that I'm unhappy with where I am in life when I play this game, it's just been a method for me to open my imagination to possibilities that may not be evident in my everyday routine. I challenge myself to think as big as possible when I'm daydreaming. I'm always surprised when I ask others to play pretend with me and notice just how difficult it is for them to open up their minds to seemingly impossible scenarios. We have to think it before we can realize it—or even move further in that direction.

When you practice creating your fantasy, don't let the voices that limit your options come into play. Take note of them and examine where and how you put a constraint on things, but continue opening to a more expanded sense of reality where anything can take place. I am aware that I have tendencies that may cause me to believe that what I desire may not happen. Therefore, it's helpful for me to practice my fantasizing in order to continue to grow that "muscle."

The next time you have the opportunity, engage a friend in the "let's pretend" game to see how creative you can be in your fantasies, or do it on your own and test your results.

45. Automatic Writing

Imagine being able to sit down and write, only to discover that what comes out of you is an inner wisdom—an answer to a situation that had not yet occurred to you. Automatic writing is sitting down to write without thinking. Sound odd? At first it might be strange, but we may be surprised at what appears on the paper. This process is a way to extract ideas that we can then apply to other creative outlets. The first time I heard of automatic writing, I was skeptical. I wondered how anything could come out of me that I would not have predicted. But it does! Many channels (people who claim to have received information from those who have passed on or exist on higher planes of consciousness) receive this information by way of automatic writing.

We too can enter into a sort of trance-like or lifted state whereby our analytical mind moves out of the way to allow a greater flow of information from our subconscious.

You will derive the most benefit from this tool by doing it habitually, especially in the beginning of your writing practice. When your mind is preoccupied it is more difficult to settle into a task. You can clear your head out first thing in the morning with some automatic writing, leaving you with a clean "slate" on which to imprint your ideas. There is no need to prepare, as the act of writing is what clears your mind. I simply sit down, take a few relaxing breaths, and let the pen flow. It's not absolutely necessary to do this exercise in the morning, but by doing it *regularly*, the exercise becomes more of a habit and therefore makes it easier to let go into the flow on the fly. You can also experiment with this key by focusing on a subject and beginning an automatic writing session that addresses that particular topic. You can do the automatic writing either on your computer or the old-fashioned way, with pen and paper. For me, the pen and paper method works best.

Enjoy the feeling of letting go into a lifted state and see what wants to emerge onto your paper. You may be surprised by the interesting data resting in your subconscious.

46. Chaos as a Creative Force

Sometimes when my office or studio is particularly untidy, I stumble upon a photo or writing or even an article that I have saved, and find myself with a new idea. I may not be able to act on it immediately, but I make note of it for future reference. Even in my bedroom, if I've not taken the time to tidy in a while, I may find a piece of jewelry I've forgotten about that could be the perfect complement to a garment I've recently worn.

We can let chaos be a destructive force, or we can let our creative choices lead us out of disorder with renewed energy for change that needs to happen. With chaos can come the unexpected, and the unexpected can bring valuable gifts, such as new perspectives. We might look to the stereotype of the mad professor, brilliance shining through in the midst of the mountains of papers piled high on a desk. You know the type: those who know exactly where a certain item hides amidst those piles also seem to have the ability to come up with ingenious ideas at any given moment.

Some personalities feel they can't function well in a disorderly environment; it's upsetting to them. I respect that we all have our preferences, but if you fall into this category try experimenting in a *small* way to see if you are able to find any unexpected gifts in an environment with less structure.

You might discover that you find creative treats in times of emotional chaos as well. Ideally, we all like to be at peace, but I have had incredible imagery arise in times of crisis or other types of emotional overwhelm. Some of my most powerful pieces of art were created out of times of grief or mayhem.

Use this key to experiment with different states of disorder to find out how you might get new creative insights. If you find yourself in a physical or emotional hurricane, step back and look at how you can create something new from any whirling bits of chaos. If we consciously make our way through the mayhem, there may be pathways to interesting creations.

47. Creative Shutdown

By beginning with where we excel, we identify a jumping-off point, an entryway where we won't be likely to get stuck. Are you aware of your strengths in regard to what you are interested in creating? Make a list of your attributes. If you have difficulty in identifying them ask a trusted friend or two for their perceptions of your talents. If you know you are good with design, volunteer to be the one to decorate the tables at an event. Reinforcing what we are good at will eventually give us the confidence to build skills in other directions. By beginning with what we know we are good at, we identify a jumping-off point, an entryway where we won't be likely to get stuck.

Conversely, are you aware of what contributes to causing a creative shutdown for you? We start to discover what forms our unique blocks to the creative process by becoming aware of triggers. Fear is at the root of whatever may give us reason for self-doubt; therefore, identifying our fears gives us information from which we can begin to build confidence. By shining a flashlight on what we are afraid of, we bring light to these fears and can do the work we need to do to help dissolve them.

Comparison shuts down more people than any other component in my experience. There will always be someone more creative, more able, better suited, and so on…We can never "win" when we compare. Trust your intuitive knowing to identify *your* greatest gifts so that you may move forward with confidence. Are you surrounded by people who appreciate what you do and support you? Or do folks who tend toward negativity, perhaps influencing you in subtle ways, enclose you? Those who dwell in victim mode, constantly complaining, drain our energy, leaving less room for creativity.

Squeezing in our creative activities either at times when we don't have optimal energy or when we don't allow a large enough window also contributes to feelings of inadequacy. Treat your project as sacred, giving it the time and fresh energy it deserves. When we show up bright and open, we have set ourselves up in the best way possible to allow in whatever brilliance wants to shine through.

Use this key to feel into what stands in the way of your progress, and create the best situations to foster, not diminish, your creative ideas.

48. Compromise

While in college, I arrived late in the semester after transferring to a different art school to find there were no available studios. I got creative and dragged my large easel and six-foot canvases out and painted in the hallways of the buildings, the only space big enough to paint the oversized surfaces I envisioned. One of my painting studios in New York City was in the basement of an old tenement that was so run-down that I did not have running water, windows, or a working toilet. I took my paintbrushes home to wash out and created some of what I consider to be my best works in the tenement studio.

Getting creative with compromise can help us achieve our goals. I've had to be flexible in order to make sure I can receive my creative and intuitive fix. For example, if I don't have the supplies that I would have ordinarily chosen and I feel the call to capture an image, be it a person, a landscape or an interior, I may have to settle for sketching and making notes that I can later translate into a painting. When I have the urge to create I make sure to honor that urge by doing whatever is necessary to follow up *while the energy is there.*

That could involve cancelling plans, changing a fixed schedule, getting up earlier, or whatever it takes to meet the muse.

Compromise is especially important in collaborations, including all of the arts. If you are asked to let go of an idea or choice of yours for the overall good of a project, it would be important to be able to intuit if this is the right choice for you. Knowing when to hold true to our own ideas involves trusting both our inner self as well as those with whom we collaborate.

If it is your ego that holds you back when you are asked to compromise, and you know that the issue at hand calls for a letting go on your end, this would be a great opportunity to practice flexibility. Projects in which you are coordinating with others such as publishers, directors, composers, are excellent tools for learning to balance your own ideas of what is important with the needs of all involved in the project. If you are being asked to let go of what you consider to be a primary aspect of a creation, call upon your intuition for ways to gracefully stick to your guns.

Compromise is an art unto itself. When we practice using intuition to learn what is right for us in various situations, we may be rewarded with greater self-confidence, as well as an ability to be flexible in ways we may not have considered.

49. The Right-Brain Experience

I often receive a puzzled expression when I mention right brain/left brain in conversations. The right-brain experience is that of being receptive. Rather than thinking or analyzing, we are more passive in order to receive. When I am painting, I am spending a lot of time in my right brain, where I find that all sorts of information, ideas, and emotions find their way in because I am so open. This receptivity enhances my painting in a couple of different ways. When I am open to emotion coming in, that emotion weaves through and is reflected onto the canvas. When I am hanging out in my right brain, I am open and I "see" additions and changes in my work that I did not plan.

Making visual art, playing music, writing or any other of the arts are excellent tools for getting the creative juices flowing. Even if we feel blocked in expressing these pursuits, we need to show up. Just like athletes work out, we can exercise and build up our creativity. Try a form of art or creative medium different from your usual activities and discover where it leads. When I put down the paintbrush and listen to music or write, I let it lead me. I can predict that one action will lead into another and another, and before I know it I am on a creative roll!

I switch back and forth from right brain to left brain as I work, enjoying being in the right brain while actually painting, then switching to left brain when I step back to analyze how the painting is coming along. In the left-brain mode, I am analyzing, critiquing, making conscious decisions about the ideas I have received and implemented while in the right-brain mode.

This movement from right brain to left brain is natural and automatic and occurs in all creative activities. Try becoming more aware of how you function from both sides of your brain to gain a better understanding of how to make the most of your own creative process.

50. Jumping In

Approaching a blank sheet of paper, a big white empty canvas, or the beginning of any creative foray can be terrifying. Some of us can't move past this first step. There are numerous ways to bypass these fears, but they all require a willingness to take at least a small leap. If I have not painted for a while and am having trouble jumping in, I like to paint over an existing painting that isn't working. A writer might try delving into a story or song written at an earlier time that could segue into a new work. Intuition can guide us to these jumping-off places.

There are a few tools I use when I have the urge to paint but don't know where to begin. My two favorites are:

1. Reviewing paintings I began but got stuck on.

2. Rummaging through my stock pile of intriguing photos in search of an image that may stimulate my imagination.

When I glance at a piece I haven't approached in a while, I will see it with fresh eyes and often know exactly what I need to do to make it succeed. After I begin making the additions or changes to that painting, I am warmed up enough to approach a new empty paper or canvas. This warm-up exercise helps me to relax into my painting process. I have also adapted this process to work with my writings.

I also keep photos in an accordion file to provide me with ideas if I need a starting point. Whenever I see or take a photo that I might like to use in a painting, I store it under the appropriate heading in the file. If the big, bad white canvas monster is intimidating me, I open the file and just flip through until I find a few that call to me. After I have selected the one I want to work with, I begin.

Another helpful tool for me is to work on more than one painting at a time. If I find myself stuck on one, I will move to another to keep the creative flow going. I know it sounds extreme, but I have been known to work on as many as four or five paintings at a time!

These tools can be applied to several other creative mediums as well.

If you are nervous and are stalling your work because you don't know where or how to begin, try some warm-up exercises elsewhere, then call upon your intuition to find what interests you most and jump in!

51. Experiment with Different Mediums

I like to work in several mediums—drawing, clay, metalwork, and more, but I'm most fulfilled by painting. If you have time constraints, before you settle on one creative activity, use your intuition to find what most excites you. If you are already committed to a particular medium or activity, try mixing in other styles to see how your current projects can be enhanced by what you learn in the other activities. We don't need to confine mixing mediums strictly to fine art. We can even consider finding the perfect set of curtains to go with a couch as mixing up the medium.

———

When I take a break from my painting to write, I receive benefits because my creativity has been exercised by using a different format. Some of what I write about gives me ideas that I want to illustrate. I combine photography and painting on a regular basis since I am inspired by working with images from "real" life. Photographing that perfect early morning mountain mist may end up in its own painting or be incorporated into one. While taking a book-making class years ago, I picked up new information about materials, such as different types of glue and papers that I used in some my collages. Any creative activity can open you up for other imaginative ventures.

Assemblage or collage is a great way to combine mediums; I can go from two-dimensional to three-dimensional. I may begin with painting and later add bits of paper, lace, feathers, bone, and more, following whatever theme I am working on. Sometimes I find that in working with these random objects, the impetus of what started out as my theme shifts, and I enjoy the creative benefits of letting go. Cutting and pasting for collage does not require any artistic background or training.

Collaborations between creatives such as visual artists, musicians, and poets can be hugely expansive. I have had an opportunity to do this on a few occasions with a poet and a musician. We used the poems as the "base" for the process. I began my part of the collaboration by studying the poem to find appropriate paintings of mine to illustrate it. The musician composed music inspired by the mood of the poem. The result was a superb combination of all these mediums in a piece that was highly effective in communicating the presentation's theme. The power of the piece was a product of our joint efforts.

My forays into other mediums have always brought more juice back to my paintings, even if it was just to switch from watercolor to oils. Shake things up for yourself and see what happens when you return to your usual ways to create.

52. Let the Work Guide You

At a certain point, a creative venture takes on a life of its own. If we are paying close attention, we can work along with the creation itself for optimum success. I love seeing the delight in my students' faces when they step away from their drawings or paintings only to discover a hidden face in a cloud or a bird in the foliage. When we are not taking space to take an overview of our project, we miss out on opportunities for magic that the work itself may bring.

What are you gravitating toward? This key comes in two parts:

1. Becoming present in the moment.

2. Using intuition to recognize the goal.

The goal is to create a sense of recognition about where or what we are being led to do. If I am so set on the way a painting has to look in the end, I am going to miss out on delightful surprises that surface naturally. Unless I am working on a very specific image for a commission, I enjoy letting the painting take part in the process too. If you set out to decorate your bedroom, for example, you may have a mood or theme that you want to create with colors in mind, but if you take it slow and pay attention as the room comes together, you will find that you may be directed to choose additional hues or accent pieces.

When writing, you probably have an idea for a story when you begin, but as you progress, you realize that the nature of one of your characters is different from what you had originally created. This person's personality dictates a change in your plot that takes the story in a whole new direction. Letting the activity take over can extend to everyday occurrences too. You may be having fun making a dish from a recipe, but if you think it would be improved with a different or additional ingredient, give it a go!

When we step out of the way and allow the magic in, we open ourselves to unexpected gifts. When our work guides us, we practice letting our creations direct us instead of holding on to fixed outcomes, and by doing this we often get more than we initially imagined.

53. Gifting

Do you find yourself standing in the aisle of a store on Christmas Eve frantically searching for the perfect gift? Or spending hours getting waylaid as you speed through different sites online? I love giving. I've noticed that most folks seem to enjoy watching as their gifts are received.

Years ago I began a practice of purchasing (better yet, creating) an item because I had an inner knowing that it would be perfect for someone in my life. I then store it in a dedicated drawer or space in my closet until I am ready to present it.

Gifting does not have to mean material things. If we are tuned in to someone, we may know that even a simple hug when they are feeling down will be received as a gift. The key is in tuning in. I remember spending a precious but very short time with a new friend on a beach. While I was taking a walk down the beach, she realized she was late to walk her dogs, but before leaving, she left a circle of sand dollars and flower petals that she placed around my chair. You can imagine my delight when I returned to this beautiful vision.

We can practice using our intuition not only in choosing ideal gifts, but in knowing when to gift. I actually prefer to surprise my loved ones with gifts at unexpected times rather than having to show up with a mandatory gift at a designated holiday. Instead, enjoy being Santa Claus on any random occasion!

54. Completion

Some artists say the most difficult thing about painting is knowing when the painting is complete. I've heard the same thing from writers. No matter what the medium, there is always more we can do to most of our creations. If you are decorating your living room, there is always one more pillow you can add for accent. This key is useful in helping to practice "tuning in" to decide whether we continue working because we enjoy the act of creation, if we can't move on or if we really are done.

We know when a piece is overworked because it loses its life—its magic. And once that happens, it's not always possible to bring it back. I require my students to step back to review their paintings every few moments to avoid overworking. With visual art, we have the opportunity to quickly review where we are as we move along. With other mediums it can be more time consuming; there are no shortcuts when it comes to listening to a complete musical arrangement or taking the time to re-read a piece of writing. Having a good sense about what we want to convey can help, unless what we are doing requires working in a more abstract or spontaneous way. In either case, we can make sure we keep things fresh.

I watch my students want to be finished with a piece when there are areas of detail to complete, such as a face on a figure, because they are too afraid of being able to paint it well. On the other hand, I watch as they overwork a piece because they are not stepping back frequently enough to view it from a distance or because they are simply enjoying the process so much that they don't want to stop.

When a project is truly complete, I experience a sense of peace within myself. If there is still more to do, I find I'm a bit anxious, not quite satisfied. If a painting is overworked, I experience the same unsettled feeling. For me, it truly is an intuiting that I call upon to determine if I am done. If I try and put the wool over my own eyes and call it done when I am not completely excited about it, I'll never be at ease when I view it.

Practice listening with your inner ears and eyes to understand when a creation or discussion is as complete as it can be at that point in time. You will know when it's time to press on if you stay tuned in without being attached to specific outcomes. This key reminds us to be sensitive.

55. Collaborate

Creativity can be greatly enhanced by joining our skills and abilities with another person. I was a hermit painter for many years, so I didn't realize how much my own creative process expands when I brainstorm with another. There is a good reason for the saying "Two heads are better than one"! Since this realization my experiences in joining forces with writers, dancers, and musicians has brought much joy and fulfillment.

In what ways can you bring in others to add to what you are creating? Are you able to take criticisms and suggestions gracefully? Even if you are working within the same medium, it can be very helpful to create a group to "roll" ideas, sounds, or other things off of. Writers' groups are very popular and visual artists get together for critiques as well. However, groups are all a bit different, so it may take a few tries to find a good fit. Groups with the right mix of personalities have certain chemistries that allow them to naturally work together better than others. Collaboration calls for patience and trust. Do you know yourself well enough to know how you will respond in a collaborative setting?

Intuition comes in handy here to help us source out those with whom we feel comfortable being vulnerable. A friend who tends to be judgmental, for example, may not be the best person to collaborate with. It's also helpful if all involved agree to share work. A discussion in the beginning of a venture where the dates and hours are agreed upon will help avoid frustrations.

It's also fun to intuit what other mediums may be a good fit for a joint project. Imagine how a collage you have created could be translated into a piece of writing or a song! Or notice how a story a friend has written may stir imagery or tunes in your head and play with those ideas. At first you may not be able to imagine the crossover (I wasn't), but it's amazing how combining talents can open up new doors and *really* get the creative juices flowing.

Find your tribe and watch your creativity soar! I love the expanded creativity that collaboration offers. Experiment with these ideas to find new ways of working with friends.

56. Inner Knowing

Self-monitoring is an art. It's okay to ask others for help. Feedback is helpful in our creative work, but we need to depend on our abilities to know what is right for us.

Are you inclined to feel secure in your decisions? Some of how we behave in regard to this key comes from our conditioning. I grew up with parents who tended to look around at what their peers were up to in many different activities, like how to decorate their homes, how to dress, where to direct their children to apply to schools—as opposed to coming up with their own ideas. Naturally, I followed the same pattern when making my choices. As I did the necessary work to help me gain confidence in life, I became more secure with my decisions. These days I may or may not ask for feedback, but I have a definite idea about what is right for me most of the time.

I took part in therapy, lived in a spiritual community, and did lots of reading in order to know myself very well. I followed different spiritual paths and took what I needed from each of them. The better I knew myself, the easier it became to feel more solid in listening to myself to know what is right for me.

Part of my process to gain confidence was to risk exposing my ideas even if there was a chance that they would not be well received. I knew that I wanted to be an artist but some discouraged me, saying I would not be able to make a living or that my illustrations were too messy. I was put on probation at Queens College because I was experimenting too much for the powers that be. Yet through all of this, I knew that I wanted to being an artist. Even as I received rejection after rejection, I kept going. I have been rejected far more times than I have been accepted.

I kept going because I knew that I had to, and perhaps you have this same knowing. When I go against the grain of what is right for me on an intuitive level, I am not at ease with myself. This key encourages you to work toward knowing yourself well in order to feel secure in your decisions.

57. Sticky Situations

It's not always easy to respond in a kind way when someone has upset or wronged us. Our intuitive faculties can source out creative responses to difficult situations to achieve what we desire without harming another. If you are unsure about how to respond to a difficult situation, invoke creativity by imagining and even writing out possible scenarios.

I often use writing as a tool when working my way through problems. I'll try several scenarios, either writing them out in longhand or on the computer to test out how I sound. We may think that we are being clear and reasonable in our communications, not realizing that we are coming across with more emotion than we want to portray. If you are not the writing sort, try verbally expressing your feelings with a friend in a practice session. You might try role-playing as a method of getting creative in finding a few different ways to express the point you want to make.

It is best not to be caught up in the emotions of a given issue when we share our view of the problem. Give yourself time to move through some of your anger or frustration before you have your dialogue. I also use my creativity to experiment with my tone. How can you best relate what it is you want to share? Are you *really* open to hearing the other person's perception of what is going on? Can you intuit whether there is an acceptance of what you are sharing?

Entering into a discussion with an open mind and attitude can set the tone for an exchange that promises a better outcome than just jumping in and demanding that the other person accept your side of the story. We can call upon our intuition to determine whether the other party understands us or when the opportune time for the discussion may be.

You can practice becoming a better communicator, even in sticky situations, through the use of the tools in this key. Your intuition is a great asset. Be sure to make the most of it, especially when you need to communicate your side of the issue.

58. *Magical Tools*

Using tools such as crystals or pendulums exercises our intuition. I recommend practicing until you are able to trust the information and understand what is right for you. Entire books have been written on each of the tools below, but the following are some basic jumping-off points.

Gemstones (Crystals)

From my observation, "crystals" are highly popular lately. What people often refer to as "crystals" are all types of rocks or gemstones. Because we know that crystals amplify energy, we can use them when we create our intentions and say our prayers in hopes that our wishes take on greater presence.

It is said that different stones work well for different purposes. Since there is much written material on stones, you have plenty of resources to help further your studies. Stones are excellent tools for working with one's intuition in making good choices. You can learn by working with yours if you feel any benefit after spending time with them. You don't have to do anything special, simply wear one in a piece of jewelry or keep one in your pocket. I have a close friend who owns a rock shop, and I've spent a significant amount of time with her as she conducts seminars about stones and on her buying trips. In the end, I trust my intuition to choose the ones I want with me, and I encourage you to also choose yours according to which ones you are attracted to.

Because I am a visual person, I tend to choose my crystals mostly because of their appearance. Others choose them for their vibration, how they feel when held. Recently I've become better at sensing which stone may be a good choice for me by way of feel, but it's subtle. There are no right or wrong choices. Here we learn to depend upon our intuition to make our best choice.

Pendulums

Using pendulums requires that we identify what our yes or no is to accurately follow that guidance in our choices. This takes some practice. Hold the pendulum still and ask a question that you know the answer to such as "Is my name Mary?" If the pendulum begins to circle clockwise you know that your yes is a clockwise motion.

Card Decks

You can use card decks as a divination tool either by asking a question and selecting a card, or by using one of the more involved card spreads such as the Celtic Cross spread. Again, there are no rules. Learn to become comfortable with the cards by choosing a deck that you are drawn to for its theme or artwork and get familiar with using it.

Magical tools are an excellent means by which we can come to depend more on our intuition for guidance. Seek out a few forms, experiment with those until you are well acquainted with them, and reap the rewards!

59. Psychometry

Psychometry is the ability to receive information from an object. In this key, we test our ability to pick up information from various items. You may discover that it is easy for you to receive information this way and can use this tool regularly as an added source for exercising your intuitive capabilities.

A fun exercise or even party idea is to ask your friends to bring an object whose roots will not be easy to trace. Place the articles in a basket and have everyone choose one with eyes closed. After choices have been made, ask everyone to get quiet and still, ready and open to receive information. Participants will then tune in and try to figure out which article belongs to whom. Some of the players will intuit by sight, and others will come to their conclusion by the way the object feels. This game is sure to start up some fun and interesting conversations.

Many folks prefer antique and thrift stores for shopping as opposed to buying "brand new." I like owning something that I know has a history. Usually I am neutral about the object, but there have been times when I simply "felt good" when wearing an old piece of jewelry. It may be that I simply feel good knowing that someone else enjoyed that piece, but it has happened that I have had flashes of people or situations when I picked up an old piece of jewelry.

Police departments have been known to call in psychics to help them solve cases. Psychometry is one of the methods those psychics use. Just as bloodhounds pick up scents, psychics pick up a "scent" of sorts by handling an article belonging to the subject of the mystery. The psychic waits to receive insight into the crime.

Becoming your own psychic detective in select situations can sharpen your insight. This activity calls in your creativity while interpreting the impressions you receive from handling an article that belongs to someone else.

60. Shifting Focus

When we are caught up in strong emotions, it can be so overwhelming that we are distracted from what we need to be doing. You can learn how to let go of the person or issue by shifting your focus to a place that will bring you into a more neutral zone. I have some suggestions on how your intuitive faculties can help in the process. When we can move away from obsessive thinking, our energy is freed up to create.

At one point, I was going through a period of grieving a loss and was so caught up in the grief that too much energy was being taken away from other areas of my life. In my despair, I created a ritual that worked a bit like the theory behind Pavlov's dog experiments, in that I re-patterned my own brain. I selected an image I had created for my *Anything Is Possible* activation card deck, one that represented moving forward without looking back. I carried that card with me everywhere so that each time I started to think about my loss, I could immediately pull the card out of my pocket or purse. I even placed a large print of it on the wall facing my bed so that it was the first and last image I saw every day. Every time I started to obsess about my loss, I immediately shifting my attention to that image and was soon able to stop grieving.

Another method to help shift focus is to give to others. Are there any people in your life that need your time or attention? It's easy to get so caught up in our own worlds that we forget to reach out when our loved ones might want or need our help. Make it a habit to take time daily to discern whether you need to allot time to another.

To have your energy available for your creations, practice shifting your focus, especially when you are suffering from distractions. Extend your creativity by devising ways to do this and you will double the fruits from this key.

61. Letting Go

Letting go can be one of our most difficult challenges, especially when it involves a loved one, a joyous time in our lives, or a pet or person who has passed away. We can practice using our intuition to bring awareness to objects that are dragging us back to the past. This action will help us let go.

Some years ago I attended a vision quest ceremony with Mary Thunder, a Native American peace elder. At this gathering, Thunder spoke of gifting things that are most precious to us. She taught us that we should learn to give away what is dearest to us as an exercise in generosity and nonattachment. To this day, when I practice giving what is closest to my heart, I remember this valuable lesson.

Sometimes it is to our benefit to let go of things that hold old energy. Objects carry memories. If we are too focused on the good old times, it might be taking away from making new ones. For example, if you are getting a divorce, new sheets may help you sleep better. Have a look around you, and if it's time to let go of an object, take a deep breath and move it along to someone you know that will enjoy it.

Let these ideas serve as a tool to help you move forward in your life by making room for *new* memories. Stretch as far as you can in terms of giving what is most difficult as your practice of nonattachment.

62. Dress Deliberately

Have you noticed that when you wear black you tend to be more "invisible" versus wearing red—which shouts *hello?* In large cities, folks tend to wear a lot of black. There may be practical reasons, such as not letting any grime from public transportation show up on our clothing, but I suspect it has more to do with protection. With so many people swarming around us there is a need for shielding, and nothing says "stay away, I'm invisible" like black. If you feel sluggish, try wearing a red garment to see if it picks up your mood. The comments from those around you may be enough to give you a lift, because folks tend to respond positively to red.

Designers look to the environment to choose colors for clothing, following the browns, rusts, and grays of autumn and winter and the lighter colors for spring and summer. I've always thought that they should reverse that pattern and offer up brighter color choices to lift our moods during the dark times.

I've noticed that I feel relaxed and trusting when I encounter someone wearing all white. In warmer climates this would not be an unusual choice, but in the middle of the winter in the cold Northeast, it can make me feel lighter to dress in the purity of white. Orange is said to be a power color. Try making this choice when entering situations where you feel intimidated. My favorite choice for public presentations is any shade of purple because I always feel good when I wear it. Others choose blue for its connection to communication. There are colors I don't look good in due to my own coloring, but if I am called to a garment of that color I trust my awareness and purchase it anyway. I then get creative about how to bring in a scarf or accessory in a more flattering color to satisfy my attraction to that color. This is a common practice for those who work with chakras and colors.

View your wardrobe with a new pair of eyes when you are feeling creative and try combining different selections that you have not considered before. Have fun seeing how others respond to your choices.

63. Pet Communication

For most people, pets are family. Pets communicate in ways that we may not fully understand, but we *do* know that they try to communicate. We can come to know by repeated interactions what our critters are conveying. In situations where I was not the only two-legged in the house, I found that my human housemates and I usually agreed on what it was that our pet was telling us. Because I've always had a strong intuitive awareness, most of the time it's easy for me to understand my critters.

There are certain traits particular to the different species that we have come to recognize. I am most familiar with cats and dogs, but especially cats, whose messages are more subtle. I have had many cats, and almost all of them will circle my feet when they want to eat or when they do their business outside the cat box if it is not up to their standards of cleanliness or if they don't feel well. I know that if one of my cats refuses to come in, it may be busy protecting my home from "threats" such as other neighborhood felines. Those activities are, for the most part, universal to cats. However, just as we are unique individuals, so are our animal companions, and if you pay close attention and tune in you will come to recognize special messages from your animal friends. One of my cats is especially possessive of me, and I get a laugh because I know his ears will go back immediately when another cat enters the room.

Are you familiar with the signals of your pets? In order to come to the best understanding, you will need to pay close attention to subtle moves and sounds. The next time your pet does something out of the ordinary, notice their ears and tail, their breathing, how they are moving (whether it is aggressively, low to the ground, etc.). Are they making sounds that are unusual for them? Have they relieved themselves in places in the home where they are not allowed? This is usually a message to master/mistress that all is not well.

Find ways of being creative to intuit your pet's communications. For example, choose the same time frame each day to be aware of what your pal is up to. Even better, choose a time when you are not with your pet and someone else is, to find out if you can feel into what your critter is up to.

Use this key to deepen your connection with your pet and practice the fine-tuning of your intuition.

64. On the Fly

As you go about your daily routine, pause to "tune in" without an agenda. When you stop your activities and fall into stillness, you become more familiar with the ability to quickly switch intuitive gears.

When we are completely present with ears and eyes wide open, we can receive inspiration. Sometimes these seemingly random, spur-of-the-moment thoughts can lead us in important directions. You have probably experienced having a conversation with someone that led you in an interesting or fruitful direction. If you hadn't listened to that inner urge to start up that particular discussion, you would not have had that experience. Your spur-of-the-moment *instinct* to begin the connection with that individual was actually a significant inner knowing. One day I was heading into town to do errands. One morning a friend and I had agreed to watch a movie that same evening. In the afternoon when I was out doing errands, it flashed in my mind to call her to disuss our options. As it turned out, she was less than a few feet away standing at an outdoor movie rental kiosk trying to make a decision about what movie to rent and had just called me for input. I said, "Wait just one minute and I'll be there." This is the kind of intuiting I'm speaking of, when we are open and available to receive, the information streams in. How perfect it was for us that we could make our selection together—the timing could not have been more perfect! This particular friend and I happen to have an outstanding psychic connection, to the point that we joke about not needing telephones, we are always so in sync.

When we are "available," we are ready to receive inspiration. This key is a reminder to stay present and available to act on your inner knowing.

65. Pay It Forward

Paying other acts of kindness forward brings a great sense of satisfaction and aligns our energy with generosity. Practice this by using your intuition to tap into whom and what to gift. Could that waitress use an extra-large tip? Should you gift one of your artistic creations to someone who needs a lift? Should you give someone a copy of your book? As an interior designer, could you donate your talents and redecorate the bedroom of a child who has cancer in order to lift her spirits? Can you give your time to mentor someone? Can you design an organization's website as a tithe? Discover the gifts that generosity can bring.

Dedicating a percentage of your income to a cause of your choice is an excellent way to make a difference in the world. Creativity enters in by way of where you choose to donate; there are so many in need of resources you may have to offer. If you don't have a budget that can support regular gifting, there are other ways to provide aid. As an artist I am frequently asked to contribute a percentage of a sale of a painting to fund-raisers for various organizations.

You might choose to serve at a soup kitchen once a week or whatever your schedule permits.

Let your intuition serve as a guide to where you may best pay it forward. Here we are reminded of how important it is to share what we have to give—our love, money, service, and creativity.

66. As in Life, So in Art

Loss is a part of the human experience. A favorite saying of mine, honoring the familiar occult and magical axiom "as above, so below," is "as in life, so in art." In a painting, I sometimes have to lose something I love for the good of the whole. I may have painted the perfect face but if it is too small for the body, I will need to re-paint it to make it work proportionately. The practice of letting go in our art helps prepare us for what we need to release in our lives and vice versa.

I repeatedly watch my painting students adamantly resist letting go of a section of their work in order to make it better. I understand only too well the feeling of having achieved exactly what I want in a section of a canvas, only to have to wipe it away because it is in the wrong position! If we take a position doing what we love to do at a job, but the work environment is toxic, we are in a similar position.

Something has to go. Are you willing to take the risk of letting go in order to create something better?

The act of stepping back from a work of art so that we can see the whole of it, reminds us that we also need to detach from what we are doing so that we may have more objectivity. When we are positioned close up to a painting, we can only look at one section at a time and we can't see how the entire thing looks together. By removing ourselves from an emotional attachment to a situation, we are better able to make intelligent decisions because we are not caught up in those emotions. Often I have to force myself to walk away from a work in progress so that I can have a clean perspective when I return. The same applies to life situations; sometimes we may need to take a break in order to see things in a different light.

As in life, so in art teaches us the value of learning from the creative process. What we encounter as we move forward in our projects can serve as a mirror to what life dishes up for us.

SPIRITUAL OR SOUL-BASED KEYS:

Establish or Strengthen Your
Connection to the Divine.

When I was in my late twenties, I experienced a profound spiritual awakening; my life would never again be the same. The events around this awakening led me to the understanding that there is more to life than what meets the eye, and I came to view the human experience differently. I have always been a seeker and was interested in the metaphysical even back then. I read everything I could get my hands on, but there wasn't much. No "New Age" bookstores existed back then, save for a couple of occult shops where I lived in Manhattan. My first mentor was a fellow waitress at the deli where I worked. I paid her $15 a session, and she taught me how to meditate and also a bit about astrology.

During this same time period I discovered that I am clairvoyant because of a frightening incident that I saw beforehand. I disliked my boss and had a dream that he had

had a heart attack and died. The next day when I arrived at work, I learned that my boss had had three heart attacks in a row and was in the hospital in critical condition. I was afraid that somehow I had caused this to happen. When I shared this with a friend, she led me to a reputable psychic who helped me understand how to use my abilities.

To that end, in addition to maintaining my daily meditation practice, I added the request to connect with my spirit guides. During a massage, I felt my first *conscious* connection to Spirit. My experience of this was a feeling of pure love focused around my throat area. It was so strong and powerful that the massage therapist felt it as well, only around my third eye area, and she experienced it as a feeling of sweetness.

I practiced connecting to this beautiful loving energy and working with it in a variety of ways too numerous to go into here, but I like to tell people my story because I am so grateful to have made a connection to the Divine. I set my intention to make this link—and followed up with the steps that led up to the above event and sustain my relationship with Spirit to this day. During that time period, I not only made a connection to the Divine but also to the core of my own being. These connections have served to deepen my creative process.

Painting is an act of spirituality for me because I am in the right side of my brain more than usual, a state in which I am most open to receive from Spirit. It feels magical to me have ideas trickle in from who-knows-where. The magic happens when I am able to translate the visions from my mind onto the canvas. If I were not as used to being in this receptive mode for extended periods of time due to my mediation practice, perhaps I would not receive as many images as I do. How I come to understand that an area of the canvas should be purple instead of blue is somewhat of a mystery, even to me. I stay quiet and when I wait long enough, the answer "appears." I observe the same process with friends of mine who are musicians and writers. Actors know when they have done a certain "take" that the magic has entered. We stay with our craft in the way we are trained to stay with our meditation training and reap the rewards of our patience with the process.

I used to paint large life-size oil paintings of anyone I found interesting. After my spiritual awakening, I felt called to begin these sessions with a ritual. In the beginning of the session, the model and I would sit together, and I would light a candle between us, say a prayer, call in our spirit guides, and sit in meditation. This made me feel more prepared to create a powerful painting by adding this ceremony into the creative recipe. By meditating together, my model and I felt more connected to each other, and it set the stage for a more intimate painting session. I continue this same ritual today every time I begin one of my Spirit Essence Portraits.

In my observations, based on both personal as well as professional conversations, I have come to understand that most people are looking for meaning in their lives—some reason for why they are here. In many cases, people want to know how they can leave their mark in a positive way in this world. We want to feel that we are contributing what we can and somehow making a difference. In this section of spiritual keys, I provide you with some suggestions to find or fine-tune direct connection to Spirit. When we are most connected to both the core of our being and source energy, we are functioning in a healthy manner, and our energy is freed up for optimum creativity. I offer intriguing ways to apply spirituality or soul-based practices to your creative process. These keys also give you ideas on applying spiritual principles to enhance or improve your individual connection to Spirit.

People who seek to connect to Spirit, God, the Divine by default find their way to more flow in their creativity. They will be less likely to find themselves in extended periods of distress. They are able to handle whatever life serves up with dignity and grace. This doesn't mean that once someone is on a spiritual path that there are no more obstacles; it means that we have the tools we need to more easily meet and accept life's challenges. We can come out on the other side of these challenges less scathed because we have learned to better cope with stress. Sound good? Let's try it!

I suggest you look to the first key, meditation, as the backbone for the rest of the keys. Meditation was what really accelerated my ability to connect with both my inner self and source energy. *If there is nothing else you take away from this book, I hope it will be that you practice whatever form of meditation that you can commit to—enjoy a greater sense of peace by going to your still point on a regular basis.*

With patience, your unique path as a creative will become more clearly defined. Enjoy the process of fine-tuning your own path to the Divine within yourself. Begin each day with connection to source, perhaps with meditation and or some beautiful soft music, and a commitment to knowing Spirit within yourself. You are your own precious gift. Love and treat yourself well and watch your creativity blossom.

67. *Meditate*

I am convinced that the single most direct way to accelerate our connection both to self and to Spirit is through meditation. With the challenges of our busy lives, the idea of meditation conflicts with our cultural programming of "got to get it done *now!*" Committing to nurturing our abilities to sit still, not think about anything and not getting anything "done" can seem foreign or unrealistic. But when we meditate, we can reach the core of our being, where creative ideas flourish, waiting to come alive. With enough discipline this can be accomplished by bringing the "tush to the cush." Even if you already have an established meditation practice, take a moment to review these insights to get ready for creative action.

Why is meditation so important you may ask? Meditation teaches us to still our active "monkey minds." When we are able to still our mind, we are able to become present in this moment, not thinking about the future nor dwelling in the past; we are simply still and *neutral*. In true meditation, we are not caught up in our emotions; we reach a beautiful serene state. Meditation offers an opportunity for peace even if we are in the midst of a deep depression or other turmoil.

There are many methods of meditating. I tend to be a purist. I learned Zen meditation, where one sits still with a straight back on the proverbial cushion, acknowledging thoughts and allowing them to drift by. The point is to *not* think, to be completely neutral. You'll be amazed by how difficult it is for even a couple of moments to pass without having thoughts. Knowing the benefits of Zen meditation,

I would be surprised if one could achieve the same results from a meditation involving listening to music or moving. Each form of meditation may be helpful, but I recommend a more formal, disciplined method of meditation. Most teachers suggest doing our meditation practice at the same time every day. I find it beneficial to consistently sit for a specific amount of time, for example, fifteen minutes to begin with, *and* set a timer. You can increase the amount of time gradually.

On the days when I meditate, I find that I am more peaceful and centered. I can glide right into my painting because I'm already present. My focus is not scattered when I go into the studio, dancing about, trying to concentrate or wasting time in emotional distress.

Explore a few types of meditation, then choose one and stick to it for a couple of months. Notice any subtle life changes that occur over time. The gifts from practicing this key—mainly peace, creativity, and clarity, are well worth your efforts. Meditation can give you the ability to handle obstacles with more grace, confidence, and clarity.

68. Creative Prayer

Regardless of our religious beliefs, most of us have asked for help from what we call God/Spirit/Source at one time or another. In prayer, we use our creative faculties, whether we realize it or not, to design our requests. Creativity in prayers helps with clearly envisioning and requesting a positive outcome.

How do *you* pray? Perhaps you recite a certain prayer that you have memorized. If so, is it possible that you may have recited the words for so long that you may no longer connect to what you are reciting? My prayers contain a basic foundation, but they are continually changing. In my Native American studies, I was taught to focus first on universal concerns, for example, for the well-being of the planet, followed by prayers for a particular culture or area in strife, followed by prayers for friends and family, and lastly for myself. *Yes*—it's okay to pray for yourself. And, I recommend you practice making the prayers for yourself as big as you can imagine.

There is no right or wrong way to pray, yet it is helpful to review how you tend to pray and consider how you can bring in a dash of creativity to switch things up. You might discover that by doing this, you can be more present during your prayer time. Try these suggestions:

+ Praying doesn't need to be limited to before bed. You can say your prayers upon waking, or at any time you feel the desire to pray.

+ When you pray, call in your spirit guides and angels or other friends in spirit for assistance.

+ Pray during movement. In kundalini yoga, prayers are integrated into the yoga postures along with visualization. You might also enjoy prayer as you walk in nature.

Use your creativity to strengthen your connection to Spirit by keeping your prayers relevant and in the moment. If you don't currently use the practice of prayer, give it a try to see how it feels.

69. Open to Spirit

It was only after I deliberately put out a call to connect with my spirit guides that I created a solid ongoing connection with them. Once we set an intention, we can create open lines of communication between ourselves and our helpers in spirit form (angels, guides, totems, or God/Spirit/Source). I "speak" with my helpers daily, especially during times of day when the veils between us are thinnest; upon waking and before sleep. This communication enriches my life.

Do you currently have a practice of connecting with Spirit, God, or whoever or whatever you think of as divine source energy? I feel fortunate that I had profound experiences with

Spirit when I was young, because those experiences changed my perspective on life and granted me a sense of connection to source energy. I can't imagine going through life without my own direct relationship with Spirit.

This connection serves me in a number of ways:

+ It helps me to have faith.

+ It helps me to know I'm not alone.

+ It helps me understand that I am never a victim, to know that whatever is happening makes sense in some way that I may or may not understand.

+ It gives me strength and confidence.

Getting Started

If you don't feel that you have a connection to Spirit or guides, angels, etc., and you would like to, I suggest you try to connect by letting "them" know that you would like to establish communication. You can speak to them out loud, but it's not necessary; you can simply send thoughts to them.

Next, you may wonder how you will know if they hear you—this will take a bit of trust. I like to ask for signs. I am often rewarded right away, by way of a special critter passing by or switching the radio to find a song that relates to my query or even a message that comes through my mind that is worded in a way that I would not ordinarily speak. Regardless of the method of response, I find that there is a *knowing* that occurs. I experience a sweet feeling along with this knowing.

Establish a line of communication and ask Spirit for ideas, direction and advice to come to you. Call upon your creativity to devise your own methods of communicating with Source energy and be ready for powerful results.

70. Gratitude

Beginning and ending each day with gratitude is a way of cleansing our souls and opening our hearts. When our "negative emotions" overwhelm us, it is more difficult to be grateful. Gratitude gives us the freedom to create!

I am in the habit of expressing my gratitude a few times a day, beginning with when I first wake up. I speak (often out loud) to Spirit and give thanks before even beginning my day. If I am entering into prayer and/or meditation, I also take that opportunity to express my thanks. I like to speak aloud each element that I am grateful for as a way of allowing myself to fully *feel* the gratitude beaming out from my heart. When I am feeling thankful, my heart is open and I experience a general sense of well-being. When I feel good, I am more likely to want to be creative than when I am down. I am also more available to others.

What role does gratitude play in *your* life? Do you tend to take things for granted or are you aware of your blessings? It's far easier to feel grateful when things are going our way. However, feeling our gratitude can be just the right vehicle to take us out of our misery as well. If I find myself getting ready for a pity party, I immediately shake myself off and mentally list what I am thankful for, and it helps! I may have to repeat the exercise a few times, but I find it to be the best tool for helping bring me back into balance. I find that folks tend to fall into two categories regarding gratitude; the whiners and the folks that realize every breath is a gift. Which category do you fall in?

Calling upon your gratitude is a practice. When this practice becomes an ingrained habit, the result is a life more filled with grace. Use this key to practice making a consistent effort to list your thanks.

71. Grace

I have often had to accept the choices gallery owners or show curators make when looking for art (when it didn't include me). Celebrating other artists' successes when I have been rejected called out a part of me that was bigger than the feelings of rejection: grace. With grace, Spirit moves through us, and we are carried to the next level of our soul's destiny.

I once heard it stated that we are only one person away from changing our destiny. I like that line. If I hadn't been rejected by each of those that turned me down, then I would not have benefitted from the results of moving forward in other significant directions. In my movement forward, I came across other opportunities and met people who helped me in other ways. I let grace come to my aid by stepping out of the way and accepting my failures in these instances. By letting my students and peers understand that I accept my rejections as part of my process, it may help them to feel better about their own disappointments.

Grace is a complex quality, real yet difficult to measure. Grace helps us to honor who we are now and who we will become by teaching us how to step aside and let Spirit move us in wonderful directions. Grace is the ability to accept defeat or challenges with dignity and pride in one's efforts, and with compassion. It's the ability and character possessed by those who win to be fair to others in victory and grateful for everything that came together to make success possible.

In our creative life, grace guides us to recognize and use our gifts in ways that will help or inspire others. Grace is often associated with elements of feminine energies such as elegance, beauty, dignity, kindness, or forgiveness.

The quality of grace is divine, as is prayer. It makes sense that we also call a prayer that we say before a meal "grace." Reflect upon how you feel when you are saying grace or any prayer. When we address the Divine, we still ourselves and become humble. Take a moment to consider a place or places in your life that could benefit from this attribute, including relationships. If we consciously call upon this trait when we are in conflict with another, we will automatically become able to dialog in a more constructive manner than perhaps previously possible.

This key can help us to connect with the power of the Divine when we can step aside and let Spirit move us. Spirit is always waiting to help us when we are willing to show up and offer ourselves with open arms.

72. The Power of Humility

Humility is a quiet yet powerful quality. When we appreciate our creation for what it is and don't have expectations about it except for the fact that the process of creating brings us joy, we experience humility. If we let our creation take on a life of its own, we honor the life of that invention.

In the past, I did many paintings because I needed to; they were strictly for my own emotional well-being. I allowed them to come through me because I needed to, and I had no attachment to having them be anything other than personal processing. They are not beautiful—in fact some of them are angry or sad—but they served a purpose. Humility allows them to rest as they are with no demands. I am fine with others viewing most of my work, but some exist strictly for my own needs, and I don't want or need to show them to others for critique or praise.

We can allow feedback from others to provide insights about what our talents have produced instead of thinking that we know it all and assume we have done a great job. Humility allows room for improvement!

If someone is humble about receiving feedback from us, we are likely to give them honest information. Often when I have been out in a public venue such as a trade show, other artists have shoved examples of work in my face when I am working my booth and paying attention to customers. Humility would instead have them ask permission to send me samples at a time when I could be more available to give them constructive feedback.

Consider how you express your humility to understand how you can continue to foster this quality. Contemplate the quiet dignity of humility. Your humility combined with respect for the privacy of others will be appreciated, and you will only enhance your own creative works.

73. The Soul and the Personality

How we celebrate our creations from a soul perspective may differ from how we experience creativity from a personality point of view. Your soul may long for the opportunity to create, and yet your personality may have something very specific to express. For me, it feels like a deep soul calling when I have the initial urge to create. It's so powerful that I actually get angry when I am not allowed to exercise that "muscle." My personality has different subjects it would like to express to the world depending upon what is going on in my life, but it's my *soul* that craves the actual act of creating.

If my soul feels especially joyful, I may call upon my personality to create a series of happy paintings depicting the reason for my joy. If I am in the throes of a new relationship, I may paint a few canvases of happy couples. If I am experiencing a loss, I may work through it via a few paintings full of sorrow. My soul creations feel like they come directly from the heart. When I am more in my head, it's my personality wanting to say something. Regardless of whether my soul or head is leading me, in those artistic expressions, I am allowing both my soul and personality to shine through by honoring my soul's need to create with expressions that satisfy my personality. This is a great exercise in balance.

Have fun feeling into whether you are creating from the soul or personality, and honor them both. Either way it's good, as long as you're exercising your ability to express!

74. Be Seen

Being in the spotlight can be terrifying. A first art show or first time onstage may be a fun, exciting experience for some, but for others, instead of joy, the stress involved brings pain and agony. In risking exposure and facing fears, the soul can find healing. Those willing to move forward emerge to honor their own creative authenticity.

I understand firsthand the feeling of safety from existing "behind the scenes." That's why it's easy for me to be a painter—that is, until it's time for an art opening. However, I've put effort into becoming more confident with allowing who I am to be seen, both in person as well as in my artwork. This has resulted in feelings of greater self-confidence that are well worth the effort. Allowing oneself to be "seen" is a process. If you can identify and face any fears that may be associated with being in the limelight, this understanding will hopefully allow you to proceed with more trust.

Consider where you might begin to practice showing more of who you are within the confines of your creative world. Any small effort will pay off. You will discover this is like working out a muscle, both in the "no pain, no gain" concept as well as the fact that the benefits show themselves little by little. When I was in art school, "figurative" (realistic) paintings were not in fashion. Abstract expressionism was all the rage, but I didn't resonate with that. I loved doing the large life-size portraits that I felt compelled to do. I knew my artistic direction wasn't "cool" like my peers' artwork, but I knew that to do anything other than what was in my heart was a self-betrayal, so I stuck with it. It took nerve to paint what was not "cool" but that was what I had to do.

I know firsthand that in showing all of who I am, I inspire others to allow themselves to be seen as well. What helped me the most in learning to take risks was being in the presence of others who weren't afraid of taking a chance and putting their creations out there. I am one who wants to face my fears; it's been rewarding coming out of the closet to grow in my ability to expose the depth of who I am. I was part of several spiritual study groups that taught me the value of showing one's true self. I was so inspired by being in the presence of others who were exposing their feelings that I chose to follow the lead of my spiritual peers.

Use this key to help inspire you to show the beauty of your creative being. Even if you don't realize you are doing it, you are helping others to get comfortable about showing their gifts as well.

75. Be Courageous

Sharing our poetry, a painting, your writing, or our views can often take courage. Awareness of our fears and accepting these fears helps us to understand ourselves better. I invite you to journey to the root of why you may have these qualms. Call in the lion of courage and dare to embrace one fear at a time, for it will lead to a freer, happier life.

Many people tend to shy away from the areas in their lives that they most fear. After all, the rare individual enjoys the panic mode. I figure I may as well do whatever it takes to face my fears because unless I find my courage, they will continue to have power over me. If I take the time to understand my fears, I can heal those places inside that need some support. When I was in my twenties, I was advised by a spiritual mentor to shine a flashlight on my greatest fears as a means to overcome them. Upon hearing that, I understood there was no other way for me. Dwelling in fear saps our energy, sometimes even temporarily paralyzing us.

Fear also contributes to missing opportunities. If we want a different job, or want to be an artist, or want a relationship but are afraid we are not good enough, we may not even try. What a waste! We all deserve to live life fully, and facing fear can help.

If you are not fully aware of what you are most afraid of, try making a list. The next time you feel your apprehension, note in your body where that fear resides. Next, breathe deeply into that place and, taking it further, send some white light to that spot. It is helpful to choose a positive affirmation statement such as "I am safe, all is well," or any other message that you create specifically for you.

Confronting our fears leads to empowerment. When we feel good, we are free once again to enjoy the creative process. Shine *your* flashlight on one particular fear. As you gain confidence, call in your creativity to approach another, and another, and another ...

76. Triggers

Our emotional triggers are the types of things that get us off balance. Certain actions and comments can immediately set us off because they touch on wounded places within us. How we *react* to triggers is a key to our well-being. I encourage you to begin to understand your own triggers and to use this awareness as a path to personal empowerment. When we are caught up in these emotional reactions, creativity is on hold, waiting for us to come back to balance.

The first step is to recognize your emotional triggers. I suggest that at the end of each day you take a moment to review if and how you had an emotional reaction to a conversation or event. Keep a written record of these instances in order to find your hidden but habitual responses. Are you able to identify a common theme in any of the times you felt upset? Some examples might be feeling left out, disrespected, antagonized, or not valued.

Next notice how you responded. Did you:

- Snap out in defense?

- Sulk away in shame?

- Retreat into a safe place inside?

- Remain balanced and not triggered by something that would usually set you off?

Don't judge yourself, simply observe. After keeping a record of this for a few days, you will notice a theme or themes that set you off. Also, in noticing how you respond, can you connect to a place in your physical body that reacts in these situations? Do you suddenly feel as if you were hit in your stomach? Does your heart hurt? Did you suddenly develop a headache? Because we store emotions in our bodies, it's helpful to be able to recognize when we are doing it so that we may allow these feelings to dissolve instead of holding on to them. If you can connect with when and where you are doing this, breathe deeply into this place and imagine sending light there.

Once you are aware of what triggers you, try digging into memories of your childhood where you find the same themes. This will help you to gain a better understanding of why you get so upset. If you can't connect to any relevant memories, don't worry; it's enough for now to identify the themes.

As you review your responses to triggers, call upon your creativity to consider whether there are more productive ways of responding in these situations. When triggers take hold of us, we are so caught up in our emotions that creativity is placed on hold. If someone criticizes your creative work, do you instantly go into a panic and take it to heart? This person's input may help your creativity blossom, but if you are caught up in old patterns of response you will miss the opportunity. We may have developed patterns that have been with us for years, but with a will to change we can take action to grow into more of the person we want to become.

Recognize your triggers to make important changes that will lower anxiety and stress. Being less bound by unproductive responses frees us up for some creative fun.

77. Embracing Vulnerability

Allowing ourselves to be vulnerable is uncomfortable. To let down our guard and open up is a courageous act. Unexpected positive rewards are yours when you are strong enough to reveal yourself.

Is there a place in your life that you can identify where you are vulnerable? If we were not given much encouragement early in our lives, or if we were punished for expressing ourselves in ways that were at odds with our parents or another authority figure, it may have become a habit to stay safe by keeping our opinions, creative ideas, and dreams to ourselves. However, when we show ourselves, we inspire others to do the same. Several years ago, I lived in a spiritual community and participated in group sharing sessions. When others were brave enough to openly share private details about their lives or their innermost thoughts, I was amazed and inspired. The courage they had to reveal so much encouraged me to make greater efforts to do the same. It wasn't easy. It's still not always easy, but with time, my willingness to be open, and at times vulnerable, has paid off.

For example, when I show my students paintings that I have done when I was depressed or angry, they are inspired to allow more of their own emotion to shine through on their own canvases. If you are involved in the arts or a career that puts you front and center, you may be more comfortable with being seen than people who are accustomed to being behind the scenes. I've had a tendency to choose to hide; I've always been most comfortable alone in my studio expressing myself on a canvas.

It's sometimes intimidating to reveal ourselves through what we have created, especially if the themes are personal. All art is somehow derived from our life experiences, so to open that up for the world to see involves taking a risk and becoming vulnerable. When I was working through a breakup of a relationship, I painted a series of very large canvases showing nude couples in various states of intimacy—not sexual but sensual. Because these paintings were so intimate, they triggered both positive and negative responses from others. I felt empowered by being brave enough to show all those parts of myself.

By becoming vulnerable, you open yourself to greater freedom of expression in both your creative and personal pursuits. There is a power in being authentic—I recommend taking the risk wherever and whenever possible.

78. Receiving

It's wonderful to be able to accept the reflection of the good that others find in us. Spirit wants us to be all that we can be. When our creations are positively received, it encourages us to keep the flow going.

How do you respond when someone compliments you? Are you likely to second-guess the comment and find a way to deny it, or do you accept it with grace? Many of us shrug off compliments because we are uncomfortable with praise. Reviewing your personal history in relation to receiving can provide you with the insight to identify reasons for any discomfort. Perhaps you were instructed as a child to be humble. It's okay to own your gifts and talents, really it is! It is not egotistical; we are not meant to diminish ourselves.

Receiving love or praise used to be very difficult for me. I've gotten better, but it is still sometimes hard for me to simply say "thank you." I know I am not alone in experiencing the awkward feelings that can come up with being complimented. Reflect upon why you feel uncomfortable. Does it feel foreign to your being? Or perhaps you may feel that if you accept those feelings you may owe that person something. There may be any number of answers to this question. I suggest taking time to remember or imagine the last time a positive expression about you felt uncomfortable. An exercise for learning more about challenges with receiving is to go into a very quiet, inner place, perhaps with your eyes closed and allow those uncomfortable feelings to arise. See if you can trace their roots. The answer may not come immediately, but eventually something should surface.

By taking in praise in relation to your creativity, you may see your talents through the eyes of another. This input can give you the incentive to hone that talent. Above all, *be proud of your accomplishments.*

79. Boundaries

Are you the one folks turn to when they have problems or feel down? It's great to be there to support our circle of friends and family, but not at the expense of our own needs. If you discover that you feel drained in any of your relationships, it's time to set limits.

Simply put, setting boundaries means saying no. I am fond of the saying "no is a complete sentence." Saying no may initially bring up feelings of guilt. Perhaps you were taught that it's right to help others—and of course it is, up to a point. If you have been caught up in this pattern for a long time, you might even believe that if you don't help such and such, then no one will—and then something awful will happen. It isn't easy to step out of the savior role, yet the rewards could be more time and energy for you and your creative projects. The trick is feeling comfortable knowing that there are some circumstances when it really is okay to say no, and other times when it is important for you, specifically, to help out.

When we don't have healthy boundaries, we waste a lot of energy—energy that could be spent elsewhere—agonizing over every request. A lack of boundaries creates bitterness, particularly if you respond in an inconsistent manner, which can distract from our chosen purpose. Having a good set of healthy boundaries frees us up to offer the world our individual gifts. Call upon your creativity to create these boundaries—once they are defined, people tend to respect them.

If you begin to change up your role of caretaker it will take some time for those on the other end to adjust. You may run into some anger when you begin to say no, but here is where your creativity can help! Finding ways to communicate in a nice way that you simply choose to opt out is liberating. The more often those on the other end receive this response from you, the less likely they will be to continue to ask. Even though it may feel cruel, you are actually healing the part of you that needs to be needed in an unhealthy way. Of course it's great to help out when you can, but doing it out of a need to feel appreciated is not healthy.

Creating healthy boundaries frees you up to have more time for your creative pursuits. It's all right to take care of yourself first—it really is!

80. Clearing

Have you ever left the company of someone and realized that you felt depleted or depressed for no apparent reason? Epsom salt baths, smudge sticks, essential oils, specific crystals, and incense are just a few tools to use to keep our space clean and clear. It's easy to pick up negative energies that make us feel drained. Those of you who tend to be extra sensitive may find yourselves more susceptible to such energies than you realize.

If you depart the company of one whose energy leaves you feeling tired or down in any way, take notice and begin to keep track of whether that is true each time you see the parties involved. You may also experience these same negative feelings when you are in particular public places.

The next time you realize that you may have been victim of a "psychic vampire," treat yourself to an Epsom salt bath. You can also use Dead Sea salts or Himalayan salts. These salts help clear our energy field, leaving us refreshed and energized. Put a good amount, maybe two cups into a tub of nice warm water and soak for about twenty minutes. Some Native American peoples have a ritual called smudging to purify the air by burning what they call their "sacreds"—sage, sweet grass, cedar, and tobacco. Most commonly they use a bundle of white sage and burn this during rituals or at any time there is a need to clean up energies. Smudging works great for me and I love the fragrance!

If you want a portable tool, purchase a bottle of spray mist that has been formulated to clear the air. I was once at a trade show and feeling tired and drained from absorbing too much energy from the crowd. A woman selling one of these sprays misted me, and I was immediate energized—and of course bought several bottles for future use. Typically, the mist will include a carrier liquid that has been infused with different crystals or oils that are known to be purifiers. Blue kyanite, black tourmaline, and other crystals known to move energy were immersed in a carrier liquid in this particular product. They may also be made from herbs or other clearing agents.

Even if our own energies may be optimal, we are subject to picking up negative energies from others. Try using some of the aids mentioned in this key to keep your own energy field clean and clear.

81. Self-Nurturing

Some of us are generous with others but stingy with ourselves. When we don't give ourselves what we need, we are less likely to feel like getting creative. Do you give yourself enough time for pleasure, recreation, or creative pursuits? Are you socializing enough? You may discover that there are patterns that need attention. For example, do you consistently spend too much time giving to others? Too much time working? Are you more likely to nurture yourself or others?

My ways of self-nurturing vary. I tend to slack off in some areas such as not taking enough time for pleasure and recreation. In other areas, I am kinder to myself, such as taking care of my physical body. Our individual needs vary so much that what nurtures me may not work for you.

Take an overview of your life and notice where there may be an imbalance. Are there any places where you are not giving yourself the attention you need? If this is true, take some time to reflect upon why you are leaving this part of your life unattended. Does giving to yourself make you feel guilty? In a way similar to being able to receive, self-nurturing is difficult if we were taught to put others first. Choose the area of your life where things are most out of balance and use this key to find ways to give yourself what you need. If you need to rest and are not taking the time to do that—pick out a movie you've wanted to see for a while and luxuriate in some laid-back decadence. Follow through by adding something else that feels inviting and notice what comes up for you after you have nurtured yourself in this way. If you managed to get through with good feelings—hooray! If it was a struggle, then you have more work to do in order to realize that it is fine to treat yourself like a king or queen. Pretend you are doing this for someone else to see if it helps.

Let this key encourage you to pamper yourself as much as you can. It may be a stretch, but you would do the same for someone else—right? Let this be a good outlet for creative, self-nurturing choices.

82. Mentor

Teaching art-making workshops is one of my favorite activities because I love seeing creativity blossom in my students. I encourage you to explore what skills you may possess to offer to others. It feels good to be of service, to be able to give of ourselves. Are there ways that you currently practice giving back to loved ones, community, or those in need of insights you have to provide as a mentor? It is rewarding to watch someone grow in a specific area in which we have expertise. When I see that person echo back what I have taught them, I know I've done my job. It feels really good to watch them achieve what they have worked so hard at—I feel like a proud mother!

If you are an instructor by profession, the content of this key will come naturally to you. Even if you are already teaching, your classes may consist of material that you learned especially for your job, and you may have other natural skills that you could also creatively apply to what your students are studying. Mentoring is a beautiful way to be of service. You don't need special skills, just a desire to get to know and help out someone who could use extra attention.

You may find unexpected ways of working with folks. For example, being an art teacher I had taken for granted that I would need to work with folks in person. Now I get creative with the internet and Skype. I give assignments based on photos that my students send me and am delighted to discover that I can make all sorts of suggestions to them to help them advance. From their completed assignments, I can see which artists may be helpful for them to look at and when it's time to try another medium. I employ lots of creativity in considering their next projects—all of this as a result of working over the internet, which I hadn't previously considered.

This key provides us with a reminder to offer our insights where and when we can. Your creativity has a lot of room to play when you find ways to share your expertise with others.

83. Patience

I am impatient by nature, but I have come to understand that patience can be cultivated. The following are some recommendations for creative ways I have learned to be more tolerant. Part of what helped me is the knowledge that I will either:

+ Achieve what it is I want.

+ I will create something better.

The key here is to practice *being present*, not looking toward the future or dwelling on the past, but having our awareness focused exactly on where we are in this very moment. In doing so, we become more aware of the subtle elements of our surroundings as well as what is happening in our physical bodies. Waiting, as a form of irritation, dissolves because we are not looking "forward"; our attention is on the present moment.

Perhaps you have some long-term goals and you are impatient about how long it is taking to realize them. Are you taking steps to move in that direction? Do you make it a habit to surround yourself with people who can provide you with ideas, inspiration, or direction? Review how you might take further action. Do something every day that gets you closer to your dream. Spend time with people who are living their dream. It's not productive to spend energy being annoyed because things are not happening quickly enough. Replace that annoyance with a positive action, even if it is a tiny step. Take it another step further and keep a log with your actions toward this goal.

When our focus is on the anger toward a situation (even if it's as simple as how slowly the line at the grocery store is moving), we waste precious energy. Shift your focus. Use these few moments to practice imagining how great it will feel to achieve a goal that you are waiting to bring to fruition or exercise your brain by memorizing a recipe in a home and garden publication. You'll find yourself much more relaxed as you leave the store.

Graceful acceptance goes a long way toward helping us realize that not all things are under our control. Relinquishing the need for control helps us to further relax into a sense of peace about the situation and opens up aspects of our creativity because our energy is not being depleted.

Call in Spirit to help you with your plans and let go and wait. As you cultivate the art of waiting, pass the time productively by doing small, yet creative, actions that get you closer to your dream.

84. Anger

Imagine being able to harness the force of anger and redirect it into your creative projects. The energy of anger is powerful and can be harnessed for creativity. We all get angry—the question is how do we best handle it? Learning to pause before we react allows time for the charge of the anger to dissipate. It is also helpful to take time to reflect upon why we may be getting angry.

You are probably familiar with the powerful feeling of anger within the body. Our heart rate goes up, our face may turn red, our adrenalin gets pumping, and we're off! You've most likely been the recipient of someone else's anger—that strong, invisible force coming at you like a psychic sword about to pierce you—not a pleasant feeling. When you think about how you feel being on the receiving end of strong negative emotions, you can understand why you may want to avoid expressing your own anger. From this perspective, you may understand how important it is to be able to work with your anger so that you are not directing it at anyone else. It's okay to have that emotion, and it's good to let the other person know that you are angry, but not with that strong energy of raw anger. Pause, reflect, *then* share how you are feeling without the energy from being caught up in "reaction mode." Your chances of being received positively are far more likely when you take the time to process before lashing out.

The next time you are mad, try going to work on something that involves your creative energy and see if you are able to transfer the energy to your creative efforts. Creative folks understand that the power of anger and the power of passion are similar. I have created entire series of paintings that were fueled by anger. Many of the paintings in my "Intimacy Sacred Erotic" series were done during a month-long artist residency that followed a fresh break up. I allowed that on-and-off relationship to drain energy from the rest of my life. I released a lot of emotion by way of putting it into my large (six-foot) canvases as well as into my tiny dream journal. The physical act of painting allowed the anger and hurt to flow out of me and onto the canvas, giving the paintings lots of feeling. Besides finding a way to heal from the hurt and frustration, and I received the added benefit of a group of powerful paintings.

I am not alone. I've had at least three students in my workshops create deep, poignant paintings while going through a divorce. And when was the last time that during a breakup you connected to a songwriter who expressed your feelings in a love-gone-wrong song? It is likely that the writer had a similar experience, which inspired the song itself.

Use this key to reap the benefits of harnessing and transmuting anger with creativity. When you sharpen your communication skills and temper your temper, everyone in your path will benefit, including (and mostly) you.

85. *Rejection*

I have become somewhat of an expert on being rejected. I tell my students that by the very nature of being artists, they will most likely receive more rejections than acceptances. Salespeople have to become experts in being rejected, but the difference is that salespeople aren't being personally rejected for their art, music, writing, inventions, and other creative projects. Rejection is hard on the ego and the heart; however, we need to be prepared to accept that our efforts will not always be received well by others. The important thing is that we do the best we can, and if we are convinced that we have done a good job, that is what is important. In our lifetime, everyone—not just artists—will experience a rejection of some sort. We can't always win. But we can pick up our paint and paintbrushes and move on to the next canvas.

Rejection brings up a lot of emotion. We may feel hurt, shame, or anger. We may feel that we are not good enough.

The reality is that *we may well be good enough*. We most likely will not know the real reasons for our rejections. There are many possibilities that may have zero to do with our talents. Perhaps those making the decisions had friends who were first in line. Maybe a different style was needed to round out demographic necessities. With so many possibilities, it would be a waste of our emotions to dwell too long on the concept that we were not "good enough" when that could be far from the truth.

It may also be true that we are, indeed, not good enough. In this case, rejection can serve as a catalyst for us to start refining our skills to become our best or moving in a new direction more suited to our skills. Ideally, Spirit works alongside us to strengthen our delicate egos through whatever means are available. If you are experiencing difficulty with emotionally processing rejection, there is always traditional therapy, but if you are not interested or don't have room for it in your budget, affordable reading material can be found in the self-help sections of bookstores specifically addressing this topic. Prayer and meditation are also useful tools to call upon to heal.

Often when I am rejected, my immediate response is anger. Sometimes when I look underneath the anger there lies hurt. After I take a good long look at the hurt, I make a conscious choice to place it delicately aside for the time being and harness the simple wave of energy of the anger as opposed to the emotion to get to an "I'll show you" (whomever you may be) and get right back to work.

It's easy to slip into victim mode when we are facing rejection. However, when we succumb to "poor me/woe is me" feelings, we are not standing in our power; we are allowing the actions of others to dictate our level of well-being. Use any tools you have mastered to help bring you back to a place of well-being so that you may return to the proverbial drawing table and pick up where you left off. I have had so many students attend my art-making classes who have been damaged by previous teachers telling them they were not talented or should not continue to pursue their artistic passions. I can relate. I was discouraged all along the way from pursuing painting as my focus in life.

If you are facing rejection, consider how much you want to achieve and what you have set out to do. If it is something you really want, use the tools in this key as a challenge to find creative ways or hone your skills to accomplish your goal.

86. Decisions

I like to blame my difficulty in making decisions on astrology since Libras are notorious for having trouble with decisions, but the truth is it has to do with fear. When we don't commit, it is usually because we are *afraid* of making the wrong decision. It's just a decision, and if the outcome is less than satisfactory, make another choice. If it is a "mistake," I will most likely learn something. In looking at it this way, nothing is really lost; in fact, something is always gained—the lesson!

When we make a decision, energy is freed up for creativity; we're not wasting time second-guessing ourselves, doing the wishy-washy dance. When we avoid decisions, we choose not to move forward, and this cuts off chances for growth. There are no wrong decisions. We choose a path and work with our choices. I am expert at speaking about difficulty with commitment; it's been a lifelong challenge.

If you are currently avoiding the commitment involved with making a decision, take time to consider any fears associated with the situation. Try journaling about it to help bring clarity, and be *honest* in your soul searching. Looking at the factors in black and white can make the issue clearer. Avoiding making decisions can be a pattern, but breakthroughs come when we begin to take risks. Usually we are not the only ones affected by not committing—others may be waiting for our decisions. I had a friend who used to pick up a menu from any restaurant we were going to so that I had time beforehand to decide what I wanted to order!

Obviously she didn't enjoy waiting for me to make a choice, but what a creative solution! I thought it was funny that she did this, but I appreciated having the time to make my choice and witnessing how my inability to make simple decisions might affect others.

Sometimes when I am having trouble making a decision, I check to see if I have looked at the "big picture." I find that if I have a good understanding of what I am deciding about I have an opportunity to engage my creativity in ways that may be a solution I hadn't yet noticed.

Use this opportunity to get in the habit of understanding your hesitancy in making a decision. You may learn that there are some common denominators among the situations that cause you to freeze with indecision. And by addressing them, you can free up your energy for more exciting pursuits.

87. Volunteer

It's part of human nature to want to contribute. We feel good when we give of ourselves. If it is difficult to find time or financial resources, we can create other ways to give or volunteer. Exploring how we can contribute is an act of creativity itself. We can open our minds to what areas call to us, then choose ways to use our skills within our selected venue. For example, if you are someone who enjoys working with food, you may choose to work at a soup kitchen, or you may contact local restaurants to ask if they are willing to donate to a kitchen or a specific fund-raising event. If you have good organizing skills, you might volunteer to be in charge of a particular benefit.

Somehow, whatever is bothering us loses power when we are focused on helping another. Being capable of identifying the needs of others helps us to more easily identify what we are grateful for in our own life. One of the best ways to lift a heavy heart is by helping someone who is having a tough time. I find that if I am feeling really bogged down and totally singing the blues, giving helps to take the focus off myself. Instead of following that predictable spiral downward, I find my way out by choosing someone or a group that I can donate my time and energy to.

Take a moment to review how you have given to others lately. Are you willing to get creative and ramp that up? If so, who comes to mind and what would you like to do for them? Consider how great you felt when a beloved was there for you in your time of need and step up to the plate for someone else!

88. Journaling

Keeping a journal is a great tool to unclutter the mind, leaving us more open to creative inspiration. We can use our journal to process thoughts and emotions. *Processing* is a term I use for digesting and understanding the events in my life. When we write down our thoughts, we are better able to see into our minds and hearts by reviewing what we have written. When I journal in this manner, I discover things that surprise me and help me grow.

You don't have to have an official journal book to write in, although I enjoy using a pretty one—somehow it makes writing in it more enticing. In journaling, refrain from censorship; just let go and write down your thoughts. Magic happens in this state of vulnerability. We are free to discover the subconscious things we were unaware of that we may want to transform.

Make journaling a regular habit and write at the same time every day if possible. If you feel awkward at first and don't know what to say, try writing as if you were writing a letter to a good friend or write: "I don't know what to write." Forget about grammar and spelling—just let the words flow. If you are having difficulty in making a decision, write about it. If you are a writer, journaling can be a way to help you stay connected with your creative rhythm, especially if you are blocked and need to stay in a routine to open up to inspiration.

After a few days of this practice, you may notice that your thoughts become more organized and your mind is less chaotic. Perhaps you discovered ideas you want to implement or remembered things that need your attention. I gain better understanding of myself by reviewing old journal entries and seeing what was going on in my life at any given point in time. Journaling enhances self-expression and allows for greater freedom of expression. Often upon reviewing my writings, I gain clarity and can move forward.

Treat yourself to a journal that expresses your personality and use process journaling to free up space in your mind, leaving more focus for creative projects.

89. Vision Board

A vision board can help you realize your deepest yearnings. When we know what our dreams are it is easier to bring them to fruition. Enjoy opening your imagination to find inspirational images for manifesting your desires, discovering new intentions and connecting to Spirit.

Think of your vision board like a collage that includes images or other visuals of what you would like to attract into your life. The most common source for images is magazines, but there are no rules. Gather your pictures wherever you can find them, maybe printing them off the internet if you want to look up a specific theme. Sometimes the reverse works for me as well; if I am looking up one thing, seeing other images might remind me of another area where I may want to place some focus. For example, if you want to call in a relationship, use images that represent what you want in your next one … like a couple laughing in bed or creating a meal together. Try to be precise in finding an image that shows the nature of a relationship that you want, one with humor, gentleness, or whatever is important for you.

Make this project fun for yourself by using your creativity to make it visually stimulating—just for *you!* Use a solid, firm backing to create your collage on, like poster board or illustration board. It doesn't have to be white—this is your creation, so go wild with it! You can paint on it, collage, paste objects, write, or do whatever excites and inspires you to keep your vision fresh.

I keep ongoing vision boards in locations that match the theme—for example a career vision board in the office. Sometimes I even have more than one. A secret to maximizing this tool for me is to place my vision boards in spots where I see them often.

My vision boards inspire and remind me to stay on track with taking the steps I need to meet my goals. Sometimes looking at it just makes me feel good and hopeful, knowing that I am clear about what it is I want. Use creativity to construct a board that will express what your heart desires. This is a wonderful tool to keep your own flame of hope glowing and to stay focused as you move toward the life you want to create.

90. Read

Reading gets our mental juices flowing and can also inspire us to discover new dreams by allowing us to visit cultures and locales that might appeal to us in ways we'd previously could not imagin.. I sometimes use my reading material as inspiration for my art and in instructive ways for my students that can also inspire my own creativity.

I divide my reading time between "serious material" to learn something (self-help, biographies, history) and fiction. Both styles charge my creativity. I always choose fiction that's placed in either a different time period or another culture so that, even then, I am learning something and/or seeing visuals in my mind. I love when I am so intrigued that I can't wait to get back to the book—that's a great book.

I am fascinated by the choices people make in what they choose to read. It says a lot about the person. Are you aware of the type of material that is most enticing to you? Do you know why you are drawn to those subjects?

Have you noticed if what you read affects you? For example, if I am very involved in a book, I find that my dreams are affected in some way by the material, either in theme, feeling, location, or other ways. Become aware of how what you are reading may weave into other areas of your life. Do you find you are having conversations about it? Does the way you choose to dress reflect what you are reading? Both of the above have been true before for me. Has it changed your perspective or are you compelled to write, paint, decorate, invent, or even cook a new recipe based on what you read?

Bring your awareness to how your reading choices are subtly influencing other segments of your life. Accept my challenge and take it a step further to experiment with deliberately making a creation after reading.

91. Create Altars

Other than painting, altars are one of my favorite opportunities to enjoy my creativity. Use altars as additional three-dimensional tools for expressing intentions for what you wish to create and as representations of what is sacred to you. You can artistically construct altars for specific purposes such as healing, attracting love, and creating prosperity similarly to how you create your vision board. Harness the power of intention to construct beautiful altars that inspire you and keep your faith strong.

You want to make your sacred spot a place that is holy for you, one that invites you to prayer and devotion. In front of my altar is most often where I formally connect to Spirit in my meditations. Get creative with selecting a suitable altar cloth. This can be elaborate or simple—again, no rules! In some traditions, an altar contains at least one article representing each of the four elements. I include the elements in any altar I construct. For example, you may place a shell or a bowl of water to represent the element of water. A candle could represent fire, a feather could signify air, and a crystal could represent the earth element. You might have a statue of a deity that is meaningful to you, perhaps a Buddha or Mary Magdalene or Yemaya. You could have photos of loved ones or homes similar to ones you would like to find, images depicting relationships, ideal jobs, good health, etc. Unleash your imagination and think as big as possible to create this sacred altar that is uniquely yours.

Perhaps the religion you were born into advocates the use of altars and you are well acquainted with them. If your associations with altars are not positive, take this opportunity to use them in a way that is highly personalized to benefit you. You may choose to have a central altar in a significant spot that will include all of the elements you are placing your focus on. Or, you can construct several different ones, specific for each issue, such as career, home, or relationship. I also recommend changing your altar when your focus changes.

Altars help you combine your creativity with your connection to Spirit. Enjoy building a beautiful center in which to focus your dreams.

92. Celebrate Your Creations

Do you allow yourself to feel joy in your creations? Can you accept that these creations are uniquely yours and that without a "you," they would not exist? If you are not rejoicing in what you have created—why not? Are you judging your creations? Do you believe that they are not that great or that someone else could do it better? Or were you taught that it is not okay to take pride in your accomplishments, that one should always be humble? Most likely, you fall into one of those categories.

Review what you have brought to fruition, large or small, and visualize how these creations have been enriching for you. If you are being hard on yourself and criticizing the results of your efforts, realize that although there may be room for improvement, you most likely did the best you could at the time. There will always be someone more competent, more organized, more talented, and so on— comparing yourself to others is not productive. If you were taught to be overly humble, consider that although those who taught you meant well, it's *okay* to feel good about whatever it is you have created. When I step back from a painting I have completed, I want that feeling of "wow, I did a great job!" It gives me a feeling of satisfaction, and I feel good showing it to others.

I celebrate my new paintings by having an open studio party toward the end of each year. When I completed my book *Painting Outside the Lines*, some friends threw a book party for me. It was like a baby shower, complete with a couple of different rituals honoring the birth of the book. The gathering was sweet; it helped me to realize that I deserved a party after all of my hard work.

Celebration helps us to realize that it is wonderful that we have put our talents to work on something; after all no one else would have done what we did in *just that way*. Celebrate *yourself and* your accomplishments!

93. Dance!

I don't care if I am dancing correctly or if I step on my partner—if I am dancing, I am happy! I realize that not everyone is as uninhibited, but I encourage you to step out onto the dance floor to discover whether you can experience the joy that I do with movement and music. I wasn't always this free with my dancing. I remember being at a wedding with my brother and sister and each of them commenting negatively on the way I moved. For years after that I was hesitant to dance in front of others. I recently met someone who used to love to dance until experiencing similar disapproving feedback, and now he still struggles to bring himself to dance at all. It takes time to feel comfortable in front of others. For me, the fun has always been worth it. Besides uplifting my spirits, dance also helps with coordination and gracefulness, which are not my strong suits! The last few years I've been doing Zumba (aerobic fitness inspired by Latin American dance that also incorporates belly dance and hip hop). I leave the sessions feeling cheerful and energized.

If music makes you feel happy, try using dance as a way to release tension, keep the body fit, and the psyche uplifted. Dance prepares us for creative adventures. Free-form dancing is a wonderful opportunity to express creativity. There are no rules in this kind of dance…just feel into the music and allow your body to express itself however it wants to without fear, without judgment. You may need to work your way up to this, but I find joy in designing moves to go with what I am listening to musically.

We can use dance to switch our energy, inspire our words, improve our coordination, or enhance our art forms. I've been known to bring my camera to dance performances to take photos to integrate into my paintings. Their costumes, poses, and the lighting have inspired a few works of mine.

Let this key inspire you to put aside your shyness and move. See just how far you can push the creative envelope using the body as your vehicle for expression.

94. Physical Movement

Our body, mind, and spirit are connected. It's a well-documented fact that exercise releases "feel good" endorphins into our system. Keep moving, especially when you are feeling the blues. My experiences with back problems taught me that often my back problems are stress-related. Consider how current stressors in your life may be linked to physical ailments you experience. Yoga and exercise are excellent ways to release tension in the body.

I've always been active and done all sorts of exercise routines, however, I have found yoga and martial arts to have the most benefits for experiencing a healthy balance of body and mind. Even though I love dance, Pilates, and a variety of other types of exercise, for me, yoga tops them all for the mental benefits I receive. If you have practiced yoga, you understand the feeling of well-being after a yoga session. I tend to feel calmer as well as "open" in a way that is difficult to describe if you haven't experienced it.

Perhaps the idea of folding yourself into a pretzel shape has you shying away from yoga. There are many different schools of yoga that are very gentle—and you can go at your own pace. Finding the right class and teacher are critical if you are just venturing into this activity. Martial arts such as Tai Chi and Qi Gong are also wonderful for strengthening the connection between body and mind. Another added benefit—if you do decide to take any type of class, or if you are visiting the gym—is that you will connect with other like-minded folk. I've formed good friendships as a result of meeting the same folk regularly, perhaps early in the morning and sharing updates on our lives. We commiserate on what a stretch it was to drag ourselves to the gym or pool so early due to all we have on our plate or how sore our bodies are from the last session. Mixing friendship with workouts makes things much more fun.

I have friends that won't "work out" but they will kayak or play tennis. When we are happy, our bodies usually reflect this and feel good. When our bodies are feeling good, more energy is freed up for our creative ventures. Use this key as inspiration to find physical activities that foster your own best body and mind connection and stick with it!

95. Feng Shui (Sacred Space)

Even if we don't know the basics of feng shui—the ancient Chinese art of placement for optimal living—we can let our imaginations soar as we employ a few simple principles. The following are some straightforward solutions to make our space ready to attract prosperity, love, family, or whatever we are seeking.

We can bring in a few basic feng shui principles to enhance all areas of our lives and without full study of this art:

+ Cleanliness

+ Keeping free of clutter

+ Color and light

+ Beauty

Have a look around your environment (including home, yard, work, and any other places where you spend a significant amount of time), and review how are the above basic principles expressed in your space.

Most of us feel better in a clean and clutter-free environment. Are you taking the time to make sure your home and your work environments are clean? If you are annoyed at yourself for not tending to this, you are wasting energy that would be better spent in creative pursuits. If you feel that you are too short on time, create *ongoing* ways of maintaining a cleaner space, like wiping off your surfaces once a day, making a commitment to put clothes away at the end of your day, or tidying up and doing the dishes every night. If you are convinced that you work well in clutter, then by all means carry on! However, if there is a lurking sense of doubt, try one big cleanup to see how you function in a tidier environment as well.

Making your space as lovely as possible is an excellent vehicle to exercise creative muscles. Make sure that you are making as much use of any natural light sources as possible by not blocking windows with furniture and maintaining well-lit work surfaces as well. Color has an important impact on our mood, so make conscious choices for making your spaces inviting, colorful, and relaxing. Sound can be relaxing; consider the addition of a simple fountain in your workspace.

If these simple feng shui ideas are successful and you feel inspired, you can study this ancient art or hire a consultant. Play with feng shui to get inspired or employ more creativity by making your environments conducive to *all* of your creative efforts.

96. Nature

Creatives throughout history have found unity with the Divine in the natural world to be a driving force in their work. The great outdoors is an easy place to connect with Spirit. I always feel closest to the Divine when I am by the ocean or in a forest.

Where is *your* place in nature? Are you a beach person? Does the purity of a fresh snowfall make you feel alive? I have a few friends who sit by local lakes and streams to write. Consider some of your favorite spots. Have you noticed any correlation between them and anything you have created or your momentum as a creator? You may have chosen a color palette for a room you were decorating without realizing that the colors were based on this location.

Being a *plein* (open air) painter takes me outside to do some of my creative work. I love being in touch with the wind, the water, the sounds, and the smells of nature as I paint. Connecting the natural world with my creative efforts is bliss. It doesn't get much better for than being able to do my creative work while outside. I end up paying a price at times, with the wind blowing my paper around or the rain threatening to wash away my picture, or my back becoming sore by sitting on hard, uneven surfaces, but usually I'm so happy and engaged with my work that I don't care. I had a musician friend who used to come out and play guitar while I painted in beautiful locations—double pleasure!

Even if I am not painting on site, nature is a constant source of inspiration. I take photos to keep images on hand for reference if I need a particular type of cloud, or wave, or another natural wonder. It's also enough for me to see a beautiful scene to want to go and paint. Beauty is at the root of much of my inspiration; beauty abounds in the natural world and fuels my creativity.

Wander outside and experience how nature can bring you closer to your experience of the Divine. Once you have made the connection, know that anytime you are stuck creatively, you can go back to a place that inspires you to recharge your creativity batteries.

97. Empowerment

Can you imagine a world filled with empowered creative people? How inspiring! How does one become empowered? When we know what we want and are willing to do what it takes to achieve that, we are on the way!

This key is similar to 92 "Celebrating Your Creations" but takes it the next step by owning your abilities as a way of standing in your power. Many women are taught that it is polite or correct to play down their gifts. Humility, in this case, does no one any good. Imagine if all the artists, musicians, and creatives denied the world what they have to share! We would miss out on all those creations. When you are clear about your strengths, make a conscious decision to use them how and when you can. In this way, you are benefitting others as well as yourself. We are all shining stars.

Empowerment requires us to take action with confidence to be who we are and to break out of any self-imposed restrictions that prevent us from living confidently and with purpose. Sometimes it is difficult to stand in our power because we have been temporarily thrown off track, perhaps due to a loss or rejection. If that is the case, ask yourself this: What can I do to get my well-being back? I begin with meditation as a first step because that brings me back into balance. For you, it may be working out to get those endorphins going or sharing feelings with a close friend. The sooner you address your feelings of being "cattywampus" (out of sorts), the easier it will be for you to right yourself again. Dwelling on our pain and anxiety doesn't serve us well.

When we reach an apex and have mastered something, those who would want to knock us off the proverbial pedestal may meet us. When we are truly empowered, we don't need anyone to tell us this is so; we continue to move ahead with confidence. It's true that early on in my career I was not confident that my artwork would be successful. I put in the hours, took what I could from many teachers, and have now reached a place where I know my work is strong even if it is not right for a certain gallery or project. To get from that point A to point B took many years and lots of effort.

Contemplate the following:

1. In what areas of your creative life
do you feel the most confident?

2. Are you using your gifts in this area?
If so, how are you doing that?

3. Are you aware of what you might be able
to do to accelerate your process? You will
know when you have arrived at where you
want to be because of your confidence level.

When empowered, we own our talents and we inspire others. Stand tall and feel the power in owning your gifts. Shine your light!

98. Self-Love

When we feel good about who we are and avoid using energy to pull ourselves down, we are happier and more likely to take on creative projects. Are you too hard on yourself? Women especially tend to be very self-critical. Self-loathing inhibits creativity. If we are busy focusing on what is wrong with us or what is wrong with our work, how can we feel good enough to create? Simple techniques can help you make a habit of being gentle and loving with yourself and give you a creative boost.

Take a step back to analyze whether or not you feel deserving of your own good loving. Trends have changed, but in my generation many of us were taught to love others but not to think too highly of ourselves. In my experience with counseling women, far too many of us find it difficult to feel love for ourselves like we do for others.

Here are a couple of tools I find especially helpful:

1. Make a list of the qualities that you appreciate about yourself. You may need to take a step back

and pretend you are someone else viewing you. If you are still having difficulty, ask someone close to you to share what they love about you. After you have your list, take a moment and imagine a mist of white and gold light surrounding an image of yourself as you state aloud each quality about yourself that you admire. Take a couple of deep breaths as you see this sweet image of you, and appreciate this feature. Continue in the same way as you make your way down the list.

2. Choose a random image of a younger version of yourself and wrap this younger one in a soft and cozy pink blanket. Ask what the younger you would like or need and imagine you from your current place in time giving the younger you a nice warm hug and providing you with exactly what you need. Ah … doesn't that feel sweet?

You can adjust this visualization to best suit your particular interests. The point is to swaddle yourself in all the gooey, sweet gushing love that you would bestow upon a newborn or a puppy! Call upon this visualization any time you feel self-doubt or loneliness, or whenever you need to give yourself some extra caring.

This key reminds us to love ourselves up! Check in to your "self-love monitor" frequently to keep an eye on any critic that may want to find a way in. Using self-love to make it a habit to embrace the beauty of who you truly are without comparison, judgment, and criticism will lead to greater self-acceptance and a more creative life. You will want all your energy for your creative pursuits.

99. Unconditional Love

This could be my favorite key—why? Because I am in bliss when I take myself to a place of unconditional love. When we connect with Spirit, it is easier to be able to feel unconditional love. From a place of pure love, we can touch on greater self-acceptance and forgiveness. The difficult practice of loving those who we dislike or are having trouble with can help us develop our ability to come from a place of love. If we can master feeling love for the ones we dislike, then maintaining this state of being with everyone becomes second nature.

Creativity enters when we imagine a different relationship with those who are a challenge to love. From here, we expand our vision or capacity to hold love beyond the present.

Many years ago, I experienced an incident that was to change my life forever. I strongly disliked my boss and had a dream that he had a heart attack and died. I went in to work the next day to learn that he had had three heart attacks in a row and was in the hospital in critical condition. I was afraid I was responsible for this. I consulted a woman who was to become a spiritual mentor and she explained to me that I was clairvoyant, that I had not caused this man any harm, but that I needed to learn to go to the place of unconditional love in order to be able to love my enemies.

Love my enemies? *What a cliché!* This took quite a bit of practice, but I learned how to go to my heart center and see this person not for their personality, but touch deeper into their soul, to realize that they are doing just what they came here to do, trigger me. Even when their behavior affects me and others in what I may initially perceive as a negative way, in truth it is a gift providing me the opportunity to learn acceptance and to be able to love that person on a soul level.

Visualize Unconditional Love

Working with the following *visualization* during meditation can be helpful:

Begin by simply calling in your spirit guides or ministering angels using a method that is comfortable for you. Tune in to your heart. Before you choose someone you are having difficulty with, it would be easiest to focus on someone in your circle of family or friends who is easy for you to love.

Connect to your feeling of love for who you are imaging; when you are "there" with them, gently replace them with the person you are having difficulty with. Imagine a beam of light shining from your heart to theirs. You may already be experiencing your fondness for them. Intensify these feelings by imagining white, pink, and gold light surrounding both of you. Bask in this light until you feel that your heart and theirs are connected. Expand that feeling of love out into the world, shining it wherever you choose. When you are well immersed in love and light, call forth the image of someone you are having trouble with and include them in your sphere.

If you find you are resisting being in this loving place with that party, return to your heart center and once again shine a beam of light from your heart into theirs.

Use your creativity to find images or thoughts that will help you to connect with that soul in a way that you may find more acceptable (for example, imagine the other person as a baby or small child). Remind yourself that this person is doing what they have come here to do—*on a soul level, not a personality level*—triggering all who were meant to be triggered in order to bring attention to areas that need to be healed. Thank that person for being who they are and triggering you so that you can find your way to heal the wound they have touched. Picture any cords of energy that may have formed between the two of you in this session being severed and each of you bringing your energy back into yourself.

Imagine if everyone in the world put forth his or her best efforts for love and acceptance in this way! This is not easy but will become easier with practice. Use your creativity in this key to find ways of making a heart connection, even with those you find difficult.

Conclusion

I've given you many intriguing ways to increase awareness and apply and use intuition in your creative process in addition to providing ideas on applying spiritual principles to enhance or improve your individual connection to Spirit. These rituals and acts, some routine and some deliberate, fuel my own waking hours and prepare me to receive inspiration in dreamtime. Through these gentle seen and unseen actions, I find my greatest joy and happiness. In showing you these secrets from my artist's canvas and beyond, my wish is that your reading of *99 Keys to a Creative Life* be used to unlock the many hidden aspects of your soul, heart, and body that support your creative nature.

For me, spirituality and creativity are always connected. In the preceding keys, I've offered you some of the ways that I have discovered to allow maximum opportunity for the creative impulse to live *through me* each day. I didn't gain this wisdom overnight; it has come to me through lifelong use of this information. If it seems like a lot, I suggest that you work with a couple of the keys at a time, integrate them into your life, then add more to your creative toolbox. I designed this book so readers could pick up a section at a time, play with what they are drawn to and/or work on things at the best pace for them as individuals. I encourage you to experiment with some of the keys and have fun incorporating them into your life to make the most of your opportunities to create.

Be patient and gentle with yourself as you continue to explore your creative process. As a reminder to key 85, rejection is a natural byproduct of being a creative of any kind. If any of your ideas are not accepted or received in the way in which you want, don't despair, continue to move forward, one foot in front of the other. If you allow another's opinion or choices to stop your creative flow and enthusiasm, you've given over your power. Stay true to what wants to emerge. The joy you feel from being free to let go and create is your reward. Tendencies to stop your projects because of negative or no response are old patterns that are no longer serving you. Rejoice in your decision to allow a greater flow of life force energy into your life by acting on your creative urges!

Aligning yourself with whatever Spiritual tools speak to you will help to reinforce each key. Even if you do not choose to move forward with more focus on your creativity by continuing to engage with Spirit you will have the tools at your fingertips to allow a greater flow of your inner creator to dance into the fabric of your life.

It's been a challenge my entire life to find ways to live outside of a typical nine-to-five work structure. I'm not made for that kind of routine, so I've had to get very creative about how to make a living as an artist and have a lifestyle that works for me. I invite you to read more about how I've done that in *Painting Outside the Lines: The Life of Psychic Artist Melissa Harris*. You may not need to make a living as an artist, but whatever you do on a daily basis will benefit from opening your inner treasure chest.

Being invited to write this book has been an honor. It's been a labor of love to examine exactly how I integrate creativity into all areas of my life, sometimes in places I originally took for granted. In a world where I've been a creative misfit, it's nice to be validated in this way. If you would like to keep in touch with me, just sign up to receive my newsletter by going to www.melissaharris.com.

These keys to creativity hold the power to bring you to a new level of inspiration, happiness, and joy. You too can unlock the gate to a more creative life. Go for it!

Recommended Resources

Access Consciousness is a website offering over 2,000 tools that you can use to change anything in your life and create greater possibilities: http://www .accessconsciousness.com

Visit Eckhart Tolle's website for understanding about how to live in the present moment: http://www.eckharttolle.com

The Emotional Freedom Technique (tapping) is a combination of ancient Chinese acupressure and modern psychology that provides ways to improve your health, wealth, relationships, happiness, and more. Nick and Jessica Ortner offer guidance for these techniques: http://www.thetappingsolution.com

Gaiam TV—Transformation Network offers access to many body, mind, spirit creativity boosting techniques and tools: http://www.gaiamtv.com

600+ free articles to inspire well-being, creativity, exploration, activate healing and joy: http://www.gatherinsight.com/freshinsights

The Global Coherence Initiative is a science-based, co-creative project launched by the Institute of HeartMath, a nonprofit 501(c)(3) and a recognized global leader in researching emotional physiology, heart-brain interactions, and the physiology of optimal health and performance: http://www.glcoherence.org

Healing with the Masters—free videos, podcasts in many areas of healing with numerous inspirational facilitators: http://healingwiththemasters.com

High Springs Emporium—rocks and minerals from around the world. Rare stones, metaphysical tools, gemstone jewelry. Classes, crystal grids for feng shui, and healings with Sharron Britton, proprietor. highspringsemporium.net

Susun Weed—Natural health, herbal medicine, and spirit healing resources. http://www.herbshealing.com

Melissa Harris Art Enterprises offers inspirational and visionary artwork, calendars, with books and card decks including: *Painting Outside the Lines—the Life of Psychic Artist Melissa Harris*; *Anything Is Possible: Activation Card Deck*; *Goddess on the Go*; affirmation card deck by Amy Sophia Marashinsky with art by Melissa Harris. http://www.melissaharris.com

The Pathwork Lectures, channeled by Eva Pierrokos, contain powerful tools for living a consciously and responsibly. http://www.pathwork.org

Ricard, Matthieu. *Happiness: A Guide to Developing Life's Most Important Skill.* New York: Little, Brown and Company, 2007.

Spirit Voyage offers tools and information including yoga, meditation, and sacred music. http://www.spiritvoyage.com

To Write to the Author

If you wish to contact the author or would like more information about this book, please write to the author in care of Llewellyn Worldwide Ltd. and we will forward your request. Both the author and publisher appreciate hearing from you and learning of your enjoyment of this book and how it has helped you. Llewellyn Worldwide Ltd. cannot guarantee that every letter written to the author can be answered, but all will be forwarded. Please write to:

Melissa Harris
℅ Llewellyn Worldwide
2143 Wooddale Drive
Woodbury, MN 55125-2989

Please enclose a self-addressed stamped envelope for reply,
or $1.00 to cover costs. If outside the U.S.A., enclose
an international postal reply coupon.

Many of Llewellyn's authors have websites with additional information and resources. For more information, please visit our website at http://www.llewellyn.com.

108 Practices to Live a
Divinely Inspired Life

Awake
in the
world

DEBRA MOFFITT

Awake in the World
108 Practices to Live a Divinely Inspired Life
Debra Moffitt

Everyone needs an anchor in this fast-paced and chaotic world. *Awake in the World* offers 108 easy ways to weave soul-nourishing peace and divinity into each day.

This engaging and practical guide was inspired by the author's own personal quest for spiritual enrichment. The practices she brought back from a journey around the world changed her life—and can transform yours. Drawn from an array of wisdom traditions, these 108 bite-sized exercises—involving meditation, labyrinth walking, inspired lovemaking, mantras, and ritual—are quick and simple to do. By sharpening your spiritual awareness, you'll learn to cultivate calm in a crisis, focus on what is truly important, and recognize the divine in everyday life. To support and encourage you on this exciting journey of self-discovery, the author shares her own personal, moving stories.

978-0-7387-2722-6, 432 pp., 5 x 7   **$16.95**

Melissa Alvarez

365 WAYS

✳

to RAISE Your

✳

FREQUENCY

SIMPLE TOOLS TO INCREASE
YOUR SPIRITUAL ENERGY
FOR BALANCE, PURPOSE, AND JOY

365 Ways to Raise Your Frequency
Simple Tools to Increase Your Spiritual Energy
for Balance, Purpose, and Joy
MELISSA ALVAREZ

The soul's vibrational rate, our spiritual frequency, has a huge impact on our lives. As it increases, so does our capacity to calm the mind, connect with angels and spirit guides, find joy and enlightenment, and achieve what we want in life.

This simple and inspiring guide makes it easy to elevate your spiritual frequency every day. Choose from a variety of ordinary activities, such as singing and cooking. Practice visualization exercises and techniques for reducing negativity, manifesting abundance, tapping into Universal Energy, and connecting with your higher self. Discover how generous actions and a positive attitude can make a difference. You'll also find long-term projects and guidance for boosting your spiritual energy to new heights over a lifetime.

978-0-7387-2740-0, 432 pp., 5 x 7   **$16.95**

To order, call 1-877-NEW-WRLD
Prices subject to change without notice
Order at Llewellyn.com 24 hours a day, 7 days a week

Daily
Enlightenments
365 Days of Spiritual Reflection

NATHALIE W. HERRMAN

Daily Enlightenments
365 Days of Spiritual Reflection
NATHALIE W. HERRMAN

Discover accessible, useful, and spiritual guidance for every day of the year with *Daily Enlightenments.* This easy-to-understand and practical handbook presents a variety of topics, including expressions of gratitude for life, challenging questions about your behavior, and dressing yourself for joy.

Each entry is a simple reminder to improve the quality of your life, and each concludes with a "take away" summary affirmation about how to best apply the spiritual concept to your life. In only five minutes of reading, this practical tool for overall well-being will ground you in a spiritual truth to improve yourself throughout each day. The accessibility and inspiration of this daily reader will bring higher consciousness to the way you do things and ultimately teach you to worry less and pursue your dreams.

978-0-7387-3712-6, 408 pp., 5 x 7   **$17.99**

"Through beautifully written vignettes and simple yet powerful reflections, Sara Wiseman helps us step into the flow of grace."
—TARA BRACH, PhD, author of Radical Acceptance

Living a Life of
Gratitude

★ ★ ★

Your Journey to Grace,
Joy & Healing

Sara Wiseman

Living a Life of Gratitude
Your Journey to Grace, Joy & Healing
SARA WISEMAN

When you walk through life with gratitude and simply appreciating everything, every single thing, you reconnect with what's truly important in life. The awe and wonder of life is now ever present.

Through 88 illuminating short stories, *Living a Life of Gratitude* will help you slow down, look around, and see your life for what it is. From our first breaths to our last, Sara Wiseman explores the landmarks of human experience: that we are able to be children and have children, that we can learn and love! Even if we have little, we have so much. Read this book, and revel in the beauty of the world.

978-0-7387-3753-9, 384 pp., 5 x 7　　　　　　　**$16.99**

THE
MINDFULNESS
HABIT

Six Weeks to Creating
the Habit of Being Present

KATE SCIANDRA

The Mindfulness Habit
Six Weeks to Creating the Habit of Being Present
KATE SCIANDRA

This step-by-step book offers a de-mystified and non-time-consuming approach to being present. It addresses the difference between meditation and mindfulness, why mindfulness is important, and dispels common misconceptions about the process. It then takes a step-by-step approach to not only teach exercises and techniques for developing mindfulness, but also includes instructions for finding the everyday opportunities to put them in place. This is done in a way that uses habit-forming principles so that at the end of six weeks, you have both a tool kit and a habit for using it regularly.

The Mindfulness Habit helps you understand the value of living in the moment and offers many ways to create the habit of finding opportunities for mindfulness. In each section of the book, you'll discover information

978-0-7387-4189-5, 216 pp., 5 x 7　　　　　　　**$16.99**
